I0415730

Issues and Knowledge Concerning the Use of Head-Up Displays in Air Transports

DOT/FAA/AR-03/50
DOT-VNTSC-FAA-00-05

Office of Aviation Research
Washington, DC 20591

U.S. Department of Transportation
Research and Special Programs Administration
John A. Volpe National Transportation Systems Center
Cambridge, MA 02142-1093

Final Report
June 2003

This document is available to the public
through the National Technical Information
Service, Springfield, Virginia 22161

U.S. Department of Transportation
Federal Aviation Administration

REPORT DOCUMENTATION PAGE

Form Approved
OMB No. 0704-0188

1. AGENCY USE ONLY (Leave blank)	2. REPORT DATE March 2003	3. REPORT TYPE AND DATES COVERED Final Report April 1998 – February 2000

4. TITLE AND SUBTITLE	5. FUNDING NUMBERS
Issues and Knowledge Concerning the Use of Head-Up Displays in Air Transports	A0825/FA0E2

6. AUTHOR(S)
Michael Zuschlag, Miwa Hayashi*

7. PERFORMING ORGANIZATION NAME(S) AND ADDRESS(ES) U.S. Department of Transportation John A. Volpe National Transportation Systems Center Research and Special Programs Administration Cambridge, MA 02142-1093	8. PERFORMING ORGANIZATION REPORT NUMBER DOT-VNTSC-FAA-00-05

9. SPONSORING/MONITORING AGENCY NAME(S) AND ADDRESS(ES) U.S. Department of Transportation Federal Aviation Administration Office of Aviation Research 800 Independence Avenue, SW Washington, D.C. 20591	10. SPONSORING/MONITORING AGENCY REPORT NUMBER DOT/FAA/AR-03/50

11. SUPPLEMENTARY NOTES
*Department of Aeronautics and Astronautics
Man Vehicle Laboratory
Massachusetts Institute of Technology
Cambridge, MA 02142

12a. DISTRIBUTION/AVAILABILITY STATEMENT This document is available to the public through the National Technical Information Service, Springfield, Virginia 22161.	12b. DISTRIBUTION CODE

13. ABSTRACT (Maximum 200 words)

This document provides a literature review of design issues encountered by the Federal Aviation Administration (FAA) during the certification of head-up displays (HUDs) for use in air transports. This review extracts certification advice from the literature and identifies research necessary to provide more complete certification guidelines for HUDs. There are four categories of design issues: information accessibility (clutter), task-display compatibility, display consistency, and physiological effects.

There is substantial research on clutter-related issues, especially with regard to interference with the out-the-window view. However, while qualitative certification advice can be drawn from these studies, there is a need for a more systematic means to determine an acceptable tradeoff between accessible flight information and clutter. There is also substantial knowledge on the task-display compatibility issues, especially concerning unusual attitude recovery. However, important benefits would be realized from the development of monochrome coding conventions for information such as alert levels. Research is needed on display consistency, especially regarding the effects of differences between the dead down and HUD layouts and formats. Likewise, the effects of HUD hardware design on pilot physiological stress and performance require study. For example, the amount of head motion a HUD must allow for is unknown.

14. SUBJECT TERMS Head-up displays, display clutter, display consistency, accommodation, aviation psychology, electronic displays, design guidelines, symbology	15. NUMBER OF PAGES 76
	16. PRICE CODE

17. SECURITY CLASSIFICATION OF REPORT Unclassified	18. SECURITY CLASSIFICATION OF THIS PAGE Unclassified	19. SECURITY CLASSIFICATION OF ABSTRACT Unclassified	20. LIMITATION OF ABSTRACT

METRIC/ENGLISH CONVERSION FACTORS

ENGLISH TO METRIC

LENGTH (APPROXIMATE)

1 inch (in) = 2.5 centimeters (cm)
1 foot (ft) = 30 centimeters (cm)
1 yard (yd) = 0.9 meter (m)
1 mile (mi) = 1.6 kilometers (km)

AREA (APPROXIMATE)

1 square inch (sq in, in^2) = 6.5 square centimeters (cm^2)
1 square foot (sq ft, ft^2) = 0.09 square meter (m^2)
1 square yard (sq yd, yd^2) = 0.8 square meter (m^2)
1 square mile (sq mi, mi^2) = 2.6 square kilometers (km^2)
1 acre = 0.4 hectare (he) = 4,000 square meters (m^2)

MASS - WEIGHT (APPROXIMATE)

1 ounce (oz) = 28 grams (gm)
1 pound (lb) = 0.45 kilogram (kg)
1 short ton = 2,000 pounds (lb) = 0.9 tonne (t)

VOLUME (APPROXIMATE)

1 teaspoon (tsp) = 5 milliliters (ml)
1 tablespoon (tbsp) = 15 milliliters (ml)
1 fluid ounce (fl oz) = 30 milliliters (ml)
1 cup (c) = 0.24 liter (l)
1 pint (pt) = 0.47 liter (l)
1 quart (qt) = 0.96 liter (l)
1 gallon (gal) = 3.8 liters (l)
1 cubic foot (cu ft, ft^3) = 0.03 cubic meter (m^3)
1 cubic yard (cu yd, yd^3) = 0.76 cubic meter (m^3)

TEMPERATURE (EXACT)

$[(x-32)(5/9)]$ °F = y °C

METRIC TO ENGLISH

LENGTH (APPROXIMATE)

1 millimeter (mm) = 0.04 inch (in)
1 centimeter (cm) = 0.4 inch (in)
1 meter (m) = 3.3 feet (ft)
1 meter (m) = 1.1 yards (yd)
1 kilometer (km) = 0.6 mile (mi)

AREA (APPROXIMATE)

1 square centimeter (cm^2) = 0.16 square inch (sq in, in^2)
1 square meter (m^2) = 1.2 square yards (sq yd, yd^2)
1 square kilometer (km^2) = 0.4 square mile (sq mi, mi^2)
10,000 square meters (m^2) = 1 hectare (ha) = 2.5 acres

MASS - WEIGHT (APPROXIMATE)

1 gram (gm) = 0.036 ounce (oz)
1 kilogram (kg) = 2.2 pounds (lb)
1 tonne (t) = 1,000 kilograms (kg) = 1.1 short tons

VOLUME (APPROXIMATE)

1 milliliter (ml) = 0.03 fluid ounce (fl oz)
1 liter (l) = 2.1 pints (pt)
1 liter (l) = 1.06 quarts (qt)
1 liter (l) = 0.26 gallon (gal)
1 cubic meter (m^3) = 36 cubic feet (cu ft, ft^3)
1 cubic meter (m^3) = 1.3 cubic yards (cu yd, yd^3)

TEMPERATURE (EXACT)

$[(9/5) y + 32]$ °C = x °F

QUICK INCH - CENTIMETER LENGTH CONVERSION

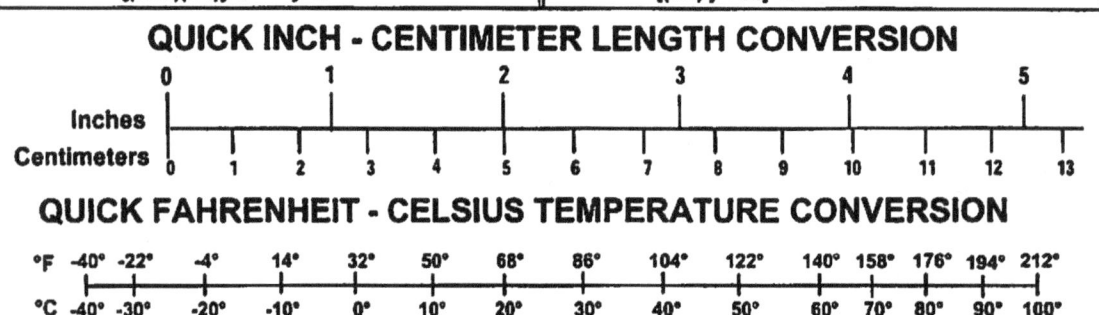

QUICK FAHRENHEIT - CELSIUS TEMPERATURE CONVERSION

°F	-40°	-22°	-4°	14°	32°	50°	68°	86°	104°	122°	140°	158°	176°	194°	212°
°C	-40°	-30°	-20°	-10°	0°	10°	20°	30°	40°	50°	60°	70°	80°	90°	100°

For more exact and or other conversion factors, see NIST Miscellaneous Publication 286, Units of Weights and Measures. Price $2.50 SD Catalog No. C13 10286

Updated 6/17/98

ACKNOWLEDGMENTS

The authors would like to express appreciation to the following people who made this document possible. Thanks to Dale Dunford, along with Sharon Hecht, of Federal Aviation Administration (FAA) Northwest Mountain Region, Transport Airplane Directorate for providing background on HUDs and the certification issues faced by the FAA. Special thanks to George Lyddane of the FAA, who also provided valuable insight on the employment and certification of HUDs.

Thanks also to Chuck Oman of the MIT Aeronautics and Astronautics Department for his continuous input and feedback on this document. We were guided to valuable information sources by Major Rick Fullmer, USAF, Bob Wood, Flight Dynamics Inc., and other members of the Society of Automotive Engineers G-10 and A-4 HUD subcommittees and the Triservice Flight Symbology Working Group and USAF Flight Symbology Development Group. Captain Becky Howell of Southwest Airlines patiently provided a detailed tour of a HUD unit aboard an operational airliner. We thank them all.

Finally, appreciation goes to Tom McCloy and Mark Rodgers of the FAA's Office of the Chief Scientific and Technical Advisor for Human Factors for their sponsorship of this project.

TABLE OF CONTENTS

TABLE OF CONTENTS (cont.)

LIST OF FIGURES

LIST OF TABLES

EXECUTIVE SUMMARY

Purpose

A research project is underway to provide the Federal Aviation Administration (FAA) with empirically based guidelines for certifying head-up displays (HUDs) for use in civil air transports. The purpose of this document, as part of this project, is to support this research by summarizing the existing literature on HUDs, providing the current knowledge and research directions for developing the certification guidelines.

HUDs are being installed in air transports in order to allow manual approaches, landings, and takeoffs in poor visibility, down to and including Category IIIA conditions. Through the course of certifying these HUDs, FAA experts have identified 22 HUD design issues each representing a potential adverse impact of a HUD design on pilot performance. In order to improve the consistency and validity of the certification process of HUDs, the FAA needs to know better, exactly how pilot performance is affected.

Display Information Accessibility Issues

Eight issues concerned the location and format design of flight information. Designers must choose what to display on the HUD, where, and how. On the one hand, pilots will have maximal accessibility to information that is displayed in the center of the HUD. On the other hand, excessive information in the HUD center or on the HUD at all likely represents clutter that slows perception of a particular information unit of interest. In order to limit clutter, the designer may simplify the appearance of a given indicator (e.g., airspeed) by omitting such elements as scale labeling, tick marks, and analog components. However, such omissions reduce the information provided by the indicator, which may lead to misperceptions.

Thus, for each unit of information, the designer must make a tradeoff between maximizing access to the information and minimizing interference with other units of information, including that presented by the underlying out-the-window (OTW) view. The literature presents no precise means to decide this tradeoff. The following rules of thumb are available for designers and certifiers:

- Only the most absolutely necessary indicators should be on the HUD.

- Keep at least the central 10 degrees of the HUD field-of-view (FOV) as clear as possible.

- All the guidelines and requirements regarding tick marks and scales that apply to the analogous head-down primary flight reference (PFR) indicators should be applied to the HUD.

- It is sufficient for a HUD to merely get the pilot's attention regarding a warning or caution while other displays describe the problem, with the exception of warnings that relate directly to aircraft attitude or control.

Further research is needed to provide more precise guidelines than above. For example, there is no technique or calculation available now, other than flight testing, that would allow a designer or certifier to evaluate systematically a proposal to locate a specific indicator at a specific location using a specific format. There does not appear to be any research indicating the degree traditional indicators can be diminished when the HUD presents unconventional indicators, such as the flight path marker and speed worm. Research on the phenomenon of attention trapping is subject to competing interpretations of the experimental data that must be resolved before design guidelines can be provided. There is virtually no research on the degree the HUD affects the likelihood of the pilot noticing important events on the head-down displays (HDDs) including cautions and warnings, although, possibly, this is not really a problem for HUDs.

Task-Display Compatibility Issues

Four issues concern the display's effectiveness to support the intended tasks. Among these, certifiers need to determine the effectiveness of the uses of symbology attributes (such as brightness, ghosting) in representing various states and values. For example, certifiers need to determine if the display adequately indicates and distinguishes commanded values and limits in altitude and speed displays, and if an indicator is out of range or has failed. According to research, X's or other overlays are preferred to removal or ghosting an indicator to show an indicator failure. Ghosting is becoming an effective de facto convention for representing an out-of-range indicator. The best use of flashing probably is purely to capture the attention of the pilot.

Regarding target values, limits, and alerts, it would seem reasonable that HUDs be subject to guidelines analogous to that applied to HDDs. Study is needed to develop guidelines for evaluating a monochrome convention for representing limits and alerts. The guidelines should identify those conventions associated with pilot performance comparable to the use of red and yellow on HDDs.

Two issues concern evaluating a HUD's effectiveness in displaying and guiding recovery from unusual attitudes. The pitch ladder symbology used in most HUDs has features that make sky-ground discrimination difficult. As a result, several differences in the positive and negative pitch ladder rungs may be necessary for a HUD to match an HDD for sky-ground recognition. Ultimately, the best approach to evaluating a HUD in this regard is flight testing.

Questions have been raised regarding the appropriateness and adequacy of various instrument formats (tape, pointer, drum, counter) in HUDs. Operational experience with HDDs suggests that to the degree that tapes have become acceptable for HDDs, one may regard them as adequate for HUDs even though counter-pointer formats may be better. Analog indicators have performance advantages over simple counters but counters alone may be appropriate when minimal clutter is necessary.

Display-Display Consistency and Discrimination Issues

Five issues concern the consistency and discriminability of HUD symbology. These concern the consistent use of coding and attributes within the HUD, discriminability of cautions from warnings in the HUD, and consistency with the formats and conventional positions of HDD indicators. There is little research relevant to these issues. While there is consensus that inconsistency should be minimized, the literature, however, does not provide guidance for deciding between two different forms of inconsistency when total consistency cannot be achieved without causing other problems.

Flight experience implies that the vertical position of the heading indicator relative to the attitude indicator can be safely varied between HUD and HDD, but no hard research supports this or other deviations from the "Basic-T" positions of indicators. Similarly, flight experience suggests it is acceptable to mix a fixed-pointer tape indicator with a round-dial moving pointer indicator. However, there are untested theoretical reasons to surmise that certain combinations of formats could cause confusion.

As mentioned earlier in this document regarding Task-Display Compatibility Issues, study is needed to develop guidelines for monochrome conventions for representing cautions and warnings. Such guidelines may address issues concerning distinguishing cautions from warnings and avoiding inconsistency with HDD alerts.

Physiological Stress Issues

Four issues concern the pilot physiological stress that may be associated with HUD optical design. These issues lack adequate research. For example, anecdotes suggest that the eye strain effects of HUDs are a possibility, although currently they are unsubstantiated. Published sources do not provide any guidance on the dimensions or characteristics of HUD optics that are related to strain or fatigue. Some research implies that pilots may shift focus when transitioning between the HUD and the OTW view. However, limitations of this research preclude any operational or design advice. HUD optics require that the pilot keep his or her head within a specific volume in order to see all flight indications. However, despite the attention applied to this issue, no one knows the normal amount of pilot head movement that would define the minimum dimensions of this volume.

Research Programs

The following research programs are proposed to aid in resolving the issues for which there is currently insufficient knowledge to provide precise guidelines for certification:

- **Visual Scanning.** The purpose of this research program is to develop a means to determine if a HUD adequately balances clutter against providing sufficient and easily accessible information to the pilot.

- **Conformity vs. Scene-Linked Symbology (SLS).** This program seeks to resolve concerns regarding attention trapping through experiments to determine if it is caused by non-conformal symbology or relative motion. Follow-up studies shall develop a measurement for a HUD's propensity to induce attention trapping.

- **Alert Coding.** Through subject matter expert workshops, technology surveys, and experiments, this program seeks to develop guidelines for evaluating monochrome coding convention for cautions and warnings in order to resolve various issues regarding consistency, discrimination, and task compatibility.

- **Internal Consistency.** This program seeks to develop a quantitative measure of display consistency that predicts human performance.

- **HDD-HUD Consistency.** This program determines the pilot performance cost (if any) associated with making the transition between a HUD and HDD when each use different formats or locations of indicators.

- **HUD Strain.** This program uses surveys and experiments to determine the presence, effects, and mitigation of strain from HUD usage.

- **Head Motion.** This program uses field tests to determine the range of normal head motion exhibited by pilots in non-HUD equipped aircraft to provide volume guidelines for cockpit head motion.

ACRONYMS

ADF........ Automatic Direction Finder

ASRS ..... Aviation Safety Reporting System

CDM ...... Climb Dive Marker

CHMV.... Cockpit Head Motion Volume

DD.......... Display-Display Consistency and Discrimination

DME....... Distance Measuring Equipment

DOT .... Department of Transportation

FAA........ Federal Aviation Administration

FOV........ Field of View

FPM........ Flight Path Marker

HDD....... Head-Down Display

HSI .... Horizontal Situation Indicator

HUD....... Head-Up Display

IMC .... Instrument Meteorological Conditions

IA .... Display Information Accessibility

ITD .... In-the-Display

MILSTD. Military Standard

MIT .... Massachusetts Institute of Technology

NASA..... National Aeronautics and Space Administration

ND.......... Navigation Display

OTW ...... Out-the-Window

PFD .... Primary Flight Display

PFR .... Primary Flight Reference

PS .... Physiological Stress

RMS .... Root Mean Square

RT .... Reaction Time

SAE........ Society of Automotive Engineers

Sim .... Simulator

SGI .... Silicon Graphics Incorporated

1. INTRODUCTION

1.1 Purpose of Document

The purpose of this document is to provide a literature review of issues encountered by the
Federal Aviation Administration (FAA) during the certification of HUDs for use in air transport.
Each issue represents a potential adverse impact of a HUD design feature on pilot performance.
For each issue, this document summarizes the current knowledge, certification recommendations
based on this knowledge, and direction of the ultimate resolution of the issue.

1.2 HUD Technology

Head-up displays (HUDs) are transparent electronic displays positioned between the operator and
the natural visual scene or out-the-window (OTW) view (See Figure 1).

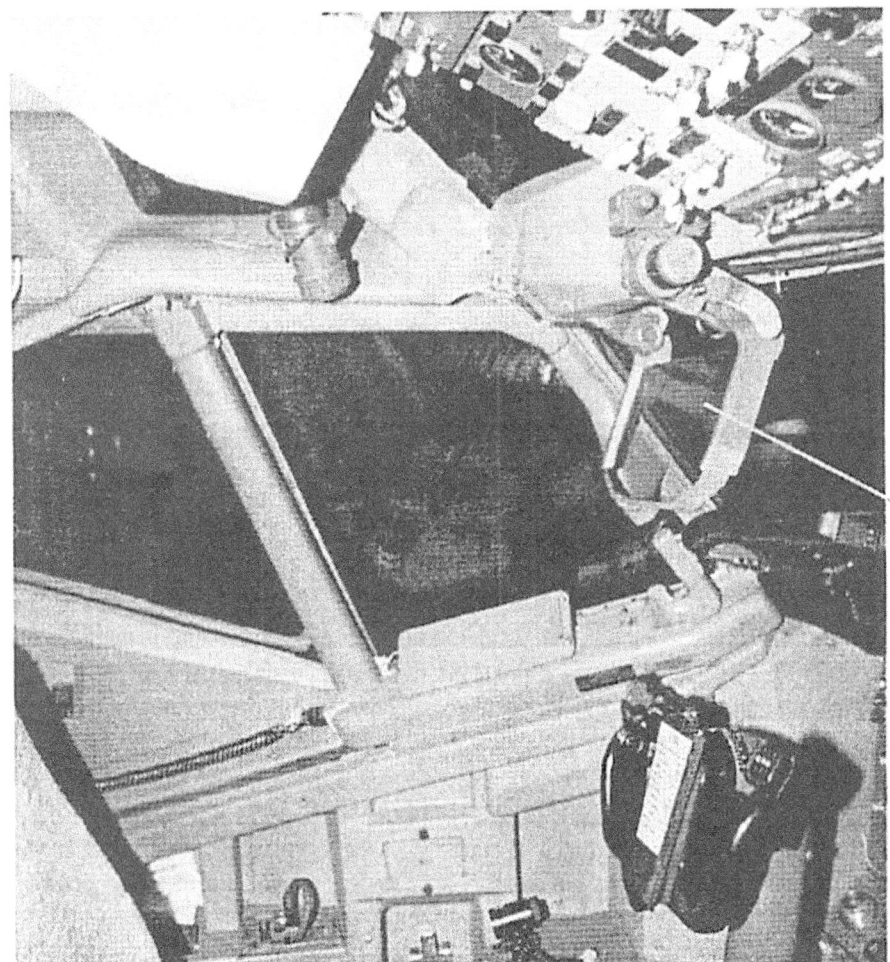

Head-up
Display

Figure 1. A Typical Civil Air Transport HUD Installation.

**The image-generating CRT is mounted overhead and the display
itself (combiner) fits in a fold-down frame**

This allows an operator to selectively attend to either the displays or the OTW view without appreciable head or eye motion. Thus, the operator can literally keep his or her "head up" for a task that requires information from both displays and OTW. This is accomplished by projecting a CRT image onto a *combiner*, being a semi-reflective panel that is typically tuned to maximally reflect the light frequency of a monochrome CRT image while allowing other frequencies of light from OTW to pass through (See Figure 2).

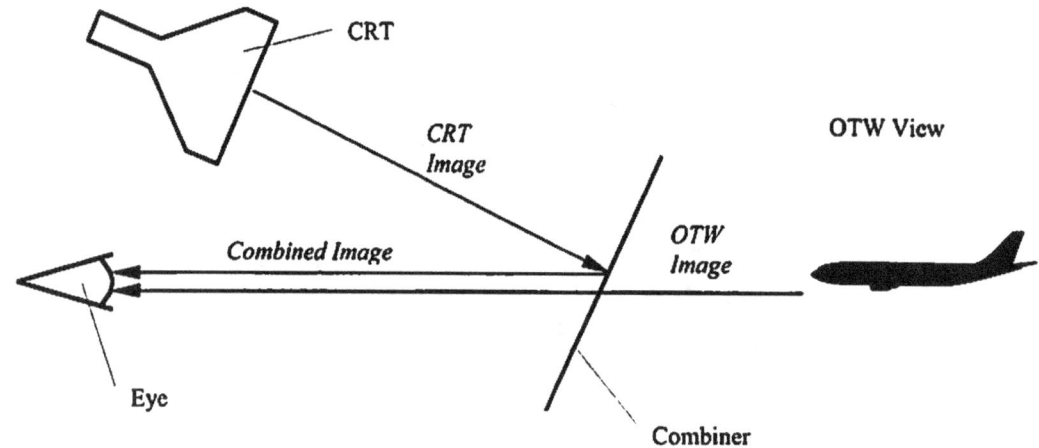

Figure 2. Basic HUD schematic, typical for civil transports.
(Adapted from Newman, 1995.)

Aviation HUDs collimate the light from the CRT, either through the combiner or separate optics. Collimation renders all light rays in parallel so that the CRT image and the OTW objects can appear in focus simultaneously.

1.3 HUD History

Head-up displays were first installed in aircraft in the 1950s to serve as electronic gunsights for warplanes (Newman, 1995; Taylor, 1990). These displays were conformal, in the sense that the gunsight's relation to the out-the-window (OTW) view corresponds with reality: when the electronic gun cross appeared on top of the actual OTW target as seen by the pilot, the weapons were properly aimed. New conformal symbology was developed in the form of flight path marker (FPM) or the similar climb-dive marker (CDM). These symbols project the aircraft's velocity vector[1] onto the OTW scene, allowing the pilot to literally see where the aircraft is going in the world outside (see Figure 3). This capacity to overlay and augment the real-world image with an electronic one proved to be the major advantage of HUDs over other electronic displays. HUDs also showed indicators for basic flight parameters such as airspeed and barometric altitude. This

---

[1] The CDM differs from the FPM in that it shows only the vertical component of the velocity vector. That is, it shows the angle the aircraft is climbing or diving with respect to the horizon, but it does not show lateral slip off the aircraft centerline.

provided a second major advantage of a HUD over a head-down display (HDD). The pilot can read key instruments while keeping the OTW view in sight, allowing military pilots to maintain focus on a target (Taylor, 1990; Weintraub & Ensing, 1992).

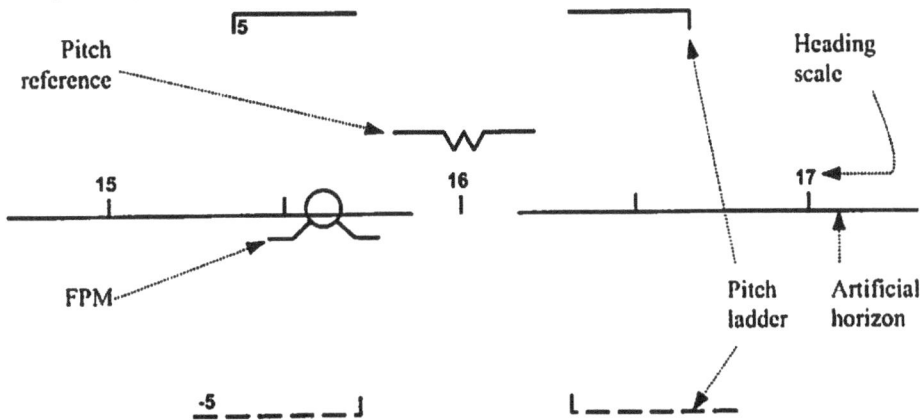

Figure 3. Representative conformal symbology.

The pitch reference indicates the aircraft is pitched up 2 degrees and heading 160. The FPM indicates the aircraft is flying a flat trajectory with a ground track of 157 (assuming the FPM is inertially based). Individual symbols are a mix of military and civil examples.

In the 1980s, analogous reasoning was applied to the use of HUDs in civil transport aircraft and the task of landing. Here, a HUD would allow a pilot to maneuver toward the runway while primary flight indications remain in view. To land an aircraft, a pilot could simply maneuver the aircraft into a heading and attitude such that the FPM lay on the end of the runway. In poor visibility, a flight path angle appropriate for an approach could be established by bringing the FPM to the proper position below the conformal artificial horizon also provided in the HUD (Newman, 1995).

With a HUD displaying a conformal flight path marker along with basic flight parameters, pilots could manually fly approaches and landings with remarkable precision (Kaiser, 1994; Weintraub & Ensing, 1992; Will, 1998). This advantage was most notable for landing in very poor visibility, when there were almost no OTW cues until flare execution. Pilot performance while using a HUD in this manner was sufficiently accurate and reliable that by 1989, HUD-equipped airliners were certified for landing in Category IIIA conditions (Kaiser, 1994; Taylor, 1990). Until then, pilots could only legally perform a landing at that visibility level by using a triple-redundant autoland system that existed in relatively few aircraft in service. The same advantages offered by HUDs for landings have also led the Federal Aviation Administration (FAA) to allow HUD-equipped aircraft to take off in otherwise excessively poor visibility.

By giving airliners the capacity to take off and land in poor visibility, HUDs acquired a substantial economic benefit for airlines that use them. Aircraft that would otherwise be subject to expensive delays or diversions are now able to keep their schedules (Kaiser, 1994; Proctor, 1997). Thus, an increasing number of airlines have been pursuing the installation of HUDs in their fleets. Industry has met this increased demand with new and innovated HUDs, all which require certification by the FAA.

Thus, HUDs, which originally were meant for targeting rather than aviating, have evolved in civil aviation to become perhaps the most important flight reference during takeoff, approach, and landing for the aircraft that have them. Recently, HUD manufacturers have also been ascribing advantages to HUDs during the cruise phase of flight. With their increasing importance, especially with regard to safety, the FAA has recognized that various design issues need to be addressed to adequately evaluate HUDs for certification.

2. STRATEGY FOR RESEARCH

In order to certify a HUD, FAA certifiers must be assured that the design features of a HUD are not implemented in such a way that pilot performance is worse than found in a non-HUD-equipped transport. A research effort is underway to develop certification guidelines to assess if a given design feature is acceptably implemented. Specifically, the research effort seeks to develop for each issue a guideline composed of a *metric* and *criterion*. A metric is a means of measuring or otherwise objectively evaluating the design implementation, and the criterion is the level of the metric the HUD should meet to be certified. In order to validate the metrics and determine the criteria, empirical studies will be conducted to determine the correlation between the metric and pilot performance. The resulting metrics and guidelines will not only aid the FAA in certifying HUDs, but will also be useful analytical tools for HUD designers who seek to minimize the impact of these issues. Furthermore, airlines can use the metrics and guidelines to aid in the selection of HUDs available from manufacturers.

This document will support this research effort by summarizing the existing literature to provide the following for each issue:

- A determination of whether the HUD design feature does indeed adversely impact pilot performance.

- An understanding of the mechanism by which the design feature affects performance, and what techniques exist to minimize the effects.

- An identification of any existing guidelines or recommendations that may be directly applied.

- A collection of potential metrics for use in evaluating a HUD.

- A collection of potential measurable forms of pilot performance that can be used to validate the metric and determine the criterion.

- A determination of requirements for additional research in addition to the development of the guideline itself.

This paper thus provides the background necessary to carry out the empirical development of guidelines regarding the issues. The methods for this development can be directly derived from here. Recommended studies are outlined in chapter 5 "PROPOSED RESEARCH PROGRAMS" starting on page 49. The most important of these studies are expected to be conducted as part of the guidelines development project that spawned this paper.

This paper also provides a general list of the most pressing FAA concerns regarding HUDs in transports and what is known about HUD design that would minimize these concerns. In summarizing the current state of knowledge regarding the human factors of HUDs in civil aircraft, this paper can thus provide interim guidance for certifiers until more empirical research is conducted.

5

3. LITERATURE REVIEW OF HUD RESEARCH

3.1 Sources

The issues themselves were derived from interviews with two FAA experts with experience in HUD certification, one expert being the FAA's Chief Scientific and Technical Advisor for Flight Management; the other being an FAA aerospace engineer with expertise in advanced flight deck displays, most particularly, HUDs. The issues thus represent the experts' opinions of the main areas where the current certification process could use the most improvement in order to more objectively and validly evaluate HUDs for certification.

The study of the issues was through a literature review of the following sources:

- Academic journals

- Symposium papers and conference proceedings

- Technical papers (e.g., NASA, Society of Automotive Engineers)

- Trade journals

- Design standards (e.g., military, Society of Automotive Engineers)

- Pilot's Guides to HUD guidance systems

3.2 Overview of the Literature

Perhaps because HUDs quietly evolved from targeting devices into *de facto* primary flight references, research has been primarily reactive to problems encountered in the course of this evolution. For example, in the early 1990s, the US military experienced an unusual number of cases of pilot disorientation in extreme attitudes for HUD-equipped warplanes. This lead to extensive research on extreme attitude recognition and recovery using a HUD, ultimately resulting in a new HUD symbology standard (MILSTD, 1996).

Of the proactive research in investigating the potential of HUDs, the tendency has been to evaluate their use in future technology such as synthetic or enhanced vision systems (Huntoon, Rand, and Lapis, 1995; Johnson and Kaiser, 1995; Leger, Fleury and Aymeric, 1996; McCann, Andre, et al., 1997; McCann and Foyle 1994; McCann, Foyle, et al., 1998) rather than for the display of more conventional indicators. Other papers have provided guidelines on conducting flight testing and evaluations of HUDs (Anderson, 1996; Anderson, French, et al., 1995; Haworth and Newman 1993).

In general, research has been most abundant in two areas:

- *Attention and Perception.* These are studies on the ability of the pilot to recognize and attend to events in the HUD and OTW, and determine the role of clutter and HUD-OTW conformity in promoting effective attention (Boston and Braun, 1996; Foyle, McCann, et al. 1995; Martin-Emerson and Wickens, 1997; May and Wickens 1995; McCann and Foyle, 1994; Sanford and Foyle, 1993; Ververs and Wickens, 1996, 1998)

7

- *Symbology Effectiveness.* These are studies that determine the effectiveness of various symbols and indicator styles for various tasks such as flight path tracking and unusual attitude recognition and recovery (Chandra and Weintraub 1993; Dudfield, Davy, et al., 1995; Ercoline, and Gillingham 1990; Liggett, Reising, et al. 1993; Weinstein and Ercoline 1993; Weinstein, Ercoline, et al., 1992; Weinstein, Gillingham, et al. 1994).

Curiously, research on attention and perception has generally excluded the relation of the HUD to the head-down display (HDD). For example, there is apparently little data on the potential that a pilot may fail to perceive an HDD event when using a HUD, and there also appears to be little data on consistency between the HDD and HUD. Also while alternative HUD symbology has been carefully studied, the hardware has not, with the exception of studies on focal accommodation. Research on head motion or eyestrain is essentially absent.

In summary, research relevant to the issues is highly variable, with some issues having copious quantities of data, and others being nearly bereft of data.

3.3 Presentation of Issues and Findings

In this document, the following is given for each issue:

- Issue *category* and identifying *number*
- *Certification need* of the issue
- Issue *importance*
- *Findings* from the literature review
- *Conclusion* based on the literature review
- *Certification Implications* derived from the conclusion
- *Future Research* necessary to resolve the issue

3.3.1 Categorization and Numbering

Issues are divided into four human factors categories shown in Table 1. Issues are sorted and numbered within each category. The numbering order is arbitrary.

Table 1. Categories of Design Issues.

Abbrev.	Category	Description
IA	Display Information Accessibility	Issues regarding the tradeoff between providing necessary information and minimizing clutter.
TD	Task-Display Compatibility	Issues regarding the display's effectiveness to support the intended tasks.
DD	Display-Display Consistency and Discrimination	Issues regarding confusion of symbols and other features both within the HUD and between the HUD and the HDD.
PS	Physiological Stress	Issues regarding the physical and/or physiological demands of using the HUD.

3.3.2 Certification Need

Each issue is described in terms of the needs of certification professionals regarding the issue. For the most part this involves determining or estimating the impact of a design feature on pilot performance. For example, for Issue IA-1, *Clutter Effects on the OTW View*, a certifier has a need to "determine if HUD's symbology excessively obscures the OTW view" in order to certify the HUD. While described in terms of a certification need, it is understood that each issue also comprises a design need. For example, for IA-1, the design need is to select and position a symbology set so that it does not excessively obscure the OTW view.

3.3.3 Importance

Issues were rated for importance by an FAA certification expert with extensive experience with HUDs using the following scale:

High   Resolution of the issue is highly critical to effectively carry out certification of current HUDs.

Medium   Resolution of the issue is important to effectively carry out certification of current HUDs, but is not top priority.

Low   Resolution of the issue would be helpful and informative for certification purposes, but it is not required to effectively carry out certification of HUDs.

3.3.4 Findings

Relevant research findings are given for each issue. Relevant research findings include any of the following:

- Findings that indicate the significance of design in the issue; that is, findings that show the degree that pilot performance regarding the issue is affected by HUD design.

- Findings that directly indicate the resolution of the issue (e.g., show what design approaches will maximize pilot performance or mitigate the impact of the issue).

- Findings that illuminate the mechanism behind the issue; that is, findings that indicate exactly what aspects of HUD design impact pilot performance.

- Findings that provide a directly applicable valid and objective guideline for certification.

3.3.5 Conclusion

The findings for each issue are followed by a summary, analysis, and evaluation of the findings with respect to good HUD design.

3.3.6 Certification Implications

Based on the conclusion, the implications for certification are described. These include any preliminary guidance that can be derived from the existing knowledge.

3.3.7 Future Research

For each issue, this document provides the research questions to be answered in order to resolve the issue. Ideally, the aim of the research is to develop validated metrics to evaluate HUD designs.

Based on the findings, there are three possibilities for future research of an issue:

- *No Research Required.* This may be for either of two reasons. (1) Any reasonably designed HUD will not adversely affect pilot performance with respect to the issue and thus no guideline is necessary. (2) While HUD design can adversely affect pilot performance with respect to the issue, an objective and valid guideline already exists that may be used for certification.

- *Metric Development Ready.* HUD design can adversely affect pilot performance with respect to the issue and enough is known about the mechanism of this effect to develop the metric and validity test to develop a guideline.

- *Research for Development.* Substantial research must be conducted before a metric can be developed. The research may be to determine if the HUD design actually adversely affects pilot performance as the issue implies. The research may also be efforts to determine the best metric. In any case, a multi-study research program is expected to be necessary to resolve this issue.

4. ISSUES AND FINDINGS

Issue IA-1 Clutter Effects on the Out-the-window (OTW) View

Certification Need Determine if HUD's symbology excessively obscures the OTW view.

Importance High

Findings In general, the detection of OTW events is as fast or faster for pilots using HUDs than for pilots using HDDs (Martin-Emerson & Wickens, 1997; Ververs & Wickens, 1996; Weintraub & Ensing, 1992). For HUDs with clutter levels comparable to that found on the market today, the effects of the HUD masking the OTW image are offset by the elimination of the need to look head down for flight displays.

However, clutter is still a concern. The display of information that is not required for the current task on a HUD has been shown to be disruptive, slowing a pilot's reaction to important OTW events such as a traffic conflict (Newman, 1995; Ververs & Wickens, 1998). Despite this finding, manufacturers will feel pressure to add content to their HUDs, potentially increasing the clutter, as pilots believe they can learn to ignore unneeded indicators as necessary. Pilots are much more likely to ask that a HUD show more indicators than fewer indicators (Kaiser 1994), not noticing that each addition may slow effective OTW visual scanning, increasing workload.

Several factors may exacerbate or ameliorate the effects of clutter:

- *Conformity.* There is some reason to believe that conformal symbology, where the symbol position with respect to the OTW view matches reality, interferes less with detecting OTW events than non-conformal symbology. (Wickens & Long, Martin & Wickens, cited in Ververs & Wickens, 1998).

- *Position.* An indicator will be less likely to disrupt the OTW view if it is placed away from where the pilot is likely to be looking, namely the center of the display or the horizon (Newman, 1995). For landing, the lower half of the HUD should be kept relatively clear of symbology so that the airport environs, ground traffic, and terrain are unobscured, and, likewise, the relatively cluttered ground texture will not interfere with the symbology.

- *Low-lighting.* There are some weak indications that low-lighting or dimming of the less essential indicators can reduce their tendency to mask OTW events (Ververs & Wickens, 1996, 1998). However, it does not appear to completely eliminate the effects of clutter.

Conclusion There appears to be a consensus that only indicators necessary for the task should be displayed. Excess indicators may delay detection of OTW events or force more careful scanning OTW, adding to workload. Being an electronic display, HUDs can add and remove indicators as needed, often automatically,

11

and indeed most HUDs on the market today do this. Manual de-cluttering modes have also been provided. However, no research has investigated how effectively pilots use such modes.

Certification Implications   Until research can provide more precise guidance, the following is recommended:

1. Only indicators and symbology that are necessary for the current task should be displayed on a HUD, where "necessary" means that the pilot must refer to the indicator or symbol repeatedly throughout the normal conduct of the task.

2. Marginally necessary indicators may be displayed on the HUD, but some combination of the following design techniques should be included to minimize their cluttering effects:

   2.1.   *Position the indicator on the periphery of the display.* The corners are especially suitable.

   2.2.   *Make the indicator conformal.* This technique should be used with caution as making some indicators conformal can have serious disadvantages such as reducing the scale to an excessively small "window."

   2.3.   *Low-light the indicator.* This should not be done if the brightness is used to mean something else in the display (e.g., an out-of-range indicator).

Future Research   Stating that one should only display necessary indicators does not exclude the possibility that the same indicators can be displayed in either a cluttered or uncluttered format. In addition to the shear amount of radiating phosphor, formats may differ in how they work in the context of typical OTW views. A particular format may work efficiently in isolation, providing sufficient information with relatively little phosphor. However, due to its specific graphic features, the same format may become lost or, conversely, may mask important OTW objects when combined with an OTW view.

The need to evaluate indicator design in context is central to resolving nearly all the IA issues. Such an evaluation procedure would need to assess both the impact of context on the indicator and vice versa. The development of this evaluation method requires long-term research.

Issue   IA-2 Clutter Effects on HUD Use

Certification Need   Determine if excessive HUD symbology prevents detection of events within HUD.

Importance   High

Findings   In findings similar to that associated with IA-1, there are definite advantages to eliminating the need to look down for an indicator by displaying it on the HUD. Events in an indicator are generally detected faster (Martin-Emerson &

12

Wickens, 1997; Ververs & Wickens, 1998) when displayed head up than head down. This is true especially in VMC conditions, when presumably the pilot is more likely to be scanning OTW (Ververs & Wickens, 1998). Tracking when using alphanumeric indicators is also improved when they are displayed on the HUD rather than on a separate HDD (Martin-Emerson & Wickens, 1997).

However, the number of indicators placed on the HUD must be limited. Pilots are slower to detect indicator events in HUDs that include indicators not needed for the task as compared to HUDs with just the essential information (Ververs & Wickens, 1998). The effect is observed when non-needed indicators are merely placed *beside* the needed indicators --it is not necessary for them to overlap. Low-lighting the nonessential information on a HUD does not appear to improve reaction time to HUD events compared to simply displaying all symbology at the same level of brightness (Ververs & Wickens, 1996, 1998).

Increasing HUD brightness may accelerate the detection of HUD events, but this will raise its contrast, and thus slow the detection of OTW events (Ververs & Wickens, 1996). Excessive HUD brightness has been associated with at least one incident in the military (Ververs & Wickens, 1998). However, it is possible to adjust the HUD brightness to a level that allows fast detection of both OTW and in-the-display (ITD) events (May & Wickens, 1995; Ververs & Wickens, 1998).

From a functional standpoint, for approach and landing, flight testing suggests that a HUD should display, at the minimum, the Basic T and vertical speed. If available and applicable, the HUD should also show lateral and vertical path deviation, the flight director, and a CDM or FPM (Newman, 1995). Some argue that the vertical speed can be dispensed with in a decluttered mode if a CDM/FPM is visible. For takeoff and go-around, the path deviation indicators, flight director, and CDM/FPM are not strictly required; however a slip/skid indicator should be added for multi-engine aircraft to cope with the possibility of an engine loss (Anderson, 1996; Newman, 1995). Other indicators (e.g., radar altimeter, speed error, etc.) may also be highly desirable (Newman, 1995). Waterline, FPM, and CDM each provide different functions making the presence of all of them desirable (MILSTD 1996).

Conclusion   It is clear that a HUD should not display indicators that are unneeded for the current task. Unlike the case of IA-1, there does not appear to be any supported means of mitigating the effects of clutter in detecting ITD events.

Certification   Until research can provide more precise guidance, the following is
Implications   recommended:

1. Only indicators and symbology that are necessary for the current task should be displayed on a HUD, where "necessary" means that the pilot must refer to the indicator or symbol repeatedly throughout the normal conduct of the task.

13

2. Candidate indicators for a HUD should reflect the likely division of labor among the flight deck crew. For example in a single HUD installation, priority should go to indicators that have no HDD equivalent (e.g., the FPM). Of indicators that would be redundant with the HDD, only indicators that *both* the first officer and captain need to monitor should be on the HUD. An important indicator for the crew task may exist only head down if it is sufficient that it be monitored by the non-HUD-using pilot alone.

3. For any task in which the pilot must continuously monitor the HUD, the HUD should at the minimum display the Basic T and some indication of vertical velocity, even if these are not strictly necessary for the task. A pitch ladder should have a waterline mark. A CDM or FPM is not an adequate substitute. A slip/skid indicator should be on the HUD in case of an engine failure in a multi-engine aircraft. This may appear automatically in such a case.

4. Marginally necessary indicators found in flight tests to be disruptive to the pilot's ability to recognize events in other more important indicators should not be displayed on the HUD, even if the manufacturer has taken the steps listed in IA-1 to mitigate their effects on masking the OTW view.

Future Research As in IA-1, clutter effects of one indicator on another are likely affected by *how* an indicator is displayed as well as *if* it is displayed. Once again, it is not sufficient to evaluate the indicator in isolation summing its phosphor usage. While that may be a good first approximation, one also needs to evaluate the indicator in context of other indicators, just as the indicator should be evaluated in the context of typical OTW backgrounds. When placed in proximity of other indicators, a particular indicator format may be relatively hard to read or, conversely, it may make the other indicators hard to read. Conceivably, there may be advantages to adding visual elements to promote perceptual separation and organization of indicators in order to reduce such interference. Ultimately what is needed is a means to estimate the clutter effects of an indicator design in context of other indicators as well as the OTW as in IA-1. This requires research for development.

Issue IA-3 Minimal Information Display

Certification Need Determine if the HUD shows the minimal information for its intended purpose, including numeric scale, tick marks, and key values as necessary.

Importance High

Findings The lack of the tick marks on a counter-pointer indicator has been shown not to affect pilot's ability to maintain level flight in turbulence (Weinstein et al., 1993), suggesting they may not be strictly necessary (Newman, 1995). However, pilots report a preference for them and theoretically the dots may result in more precision in maintaining a commanded airspeed (MILSTD

14

1996). Thus, at least for pointer-counter airspeed and altitude indicator, tick marks have been recommended, but it has also been recommended that they be barely visible in order to minimize clutter (Newman, 1995).

Development work by the US Air Force has lead to recommendations that HUDs show the currently selected altitude and airspeed on their respective indicators, consistent with conventions for HDDs (Federal Aviation Administration, 1987). When these values are out of range of the analogue indicator, they may be displayed above or below the indicator (Newman, 1995; MILSTD 1996). The following reference speeds are recommended for takeoff: V_1, rotate speed, and V_2. These may be removed after liftoff (Newman, 1995; MILSTD 1996). The display should also show speed limits, such as never-exceed and stall speeds for the aircraft's current configuration or, alternatively, reference speeds for gear and flaps (MILSTD 1996).

General human factors standards recommend avoiding irregular tick marks and insufficient value labeling as they are associated with poor performance in identifying a displayed value (Kantowitz & Sorkin, 1983; Woodson, et al., 1992). An important function of an analogue display is to provide rate-of-change feedback (Kantowitz & Sorkin, 1983). Any kind of nonlinear scale can be expected to interfere with this. Analog airspeed indicators have been know to use different linear scales for different speed ranges, but in this case potential interference may be ameliorated by changing the scales at meaningful breaks in speeds (e.g., below minimal V_1 and at 250 kts.). Tests indicate that the pitch ladder of a HUD may also be dual scaled or even nonlinear in order to provide compression at extreme pitches for improved performance in recovering from unusual attitudes (Newman, 1995). In an unusual attitude precise modulation of the rate of pitch change is not likely to be the pilot's main concern. In general there is a lack of research on nonlinear scales in an aviation context.

Conclusion   It should be generally assumed that the indicators on the HUD will be the primary reference for the pilot while the HUD is in use. Thus, all the guidelines and requirements that apply to analogous head-down PFR indicators should be applied to the HUD. For example, if a reference speed is required on the PFD, then it should also be shown on the HUD. At this time there is no research that indicates that HUDs that are used as primary reference perform adequately with less than all the information required for a HDD PFR.

Scale nonlinearity is generally not recommended for displays. In particular, it would be difficult to justify any use of nonlinearity for airspeed or altitude where rate of change is nearly always a concern and often the primary justification for providing an analogue component for the indicator. However, changing scales for different ranges while maintaining linearity within each range is not necessarily harmful.

While Weinstein et al. (1993) failed to show that tick marks improve performance on HUDs over no tick marks, this lack of result may have been

15

limited to particular combination of task and indicator design they used (e.g., round dial, a single linear scale, no tick mark labels). The general opinion among experts is that tick marks have sufficient advantages to justify displaying them.

Certification Implications The following guidelines are given pending further research:

1. Analogue indicators should display counters, value labels, or such so that the pilot can quickly and unambiguously identify the displayed value.

2. The Basic-T indicators on the HUD should display the same information (e.g., commanded and reference values) as required for analogous HDD indicators.

3. Additional information beyond that in the Basic-T may also be shown on the HUD if adding clutter is justified by improved pilot performance (e.g., to prevent breaking visual lock on the runaway on flare).

4. Analogue indicators such as airspeed and altitude that may require tracking by the pilot should have tick marks, but these should be small and unobtrusive (e.g., small dots).

5. Nonlinear scales should not be used for airspeed and altitude. At the very least, flight testing should carefully evaluate the pilot's ability to control the approach to various target or limit values when nonlinear scales are used.

Future Research The effect of labeling the tick marks, as is conventional for airspeed indicators and altimeters (Federal Aviation Administration, 1987), has apparently not been fully evaluated in HUDs and may or may not be associated with improved performance. Nor have variations of indicator format been compared on tasks other than tracking a constant airspeed and altitude, such as awareness of an approaching performance limit (e.g., accelerating towards V_{MO} or descending towards the MDA). Also, evaluations of certain formats such as moving pointer linear displays have apparently not been published.

If all the guidelines that apply to HDD indicators should also apply to HUD indicators, one may therefore argue that no additional research is called for, and the research and experience with ordinary indicators should be applied to HUDs. The HUD's transparency and redundancy with the HDD (monitored by the non-HUD-using pilot), however, implies that indicator elements that are desirable in an HDD may not be desirable in a HUD. Ticks marks labels, for example, may be desirable in an HDD, where the benefits of information outweigh the clutter, but this may not be so in a HUD. This implies that this issue is very similar to IA-2, raising the same question of what information needs to be head-up. The research for development of metrics for Issues IA-1 and IA-2 could thus also be used to resolve IA-3.

Specifically, the importance of tick marks for various analog HUD indicators remains an open question. In particular, research is need to assess potential performance benefits associated with acquiring (rather than merely

16

maintaining) target values and remaining within limits. Possibly the presence of tick marks may yield a measurable improvement over their absence in round dial indicators when the tick marks are labeled.

Issue **IA-4** Centrality of Indicators

Certification Need Determine if flight indications are sufficiently close to the center of the pilot's vision to allow detection of events.

Importance Medium

Findings As a general human factors principle, events on centrally located indicators are detected with less effort than those on peripherally located indicators and training is necessary to elicit effective scanning of peripherally located indicators (Kantowitz & Sorkin, 1983). In a HUD in particular, the collimating optics make it more likely that indicators on the periphery will fall outside the field of view due to normal head motion (see PS-3). Designers must avoid placing an indicator that may show an abnormal or hazardous condition where it can drop out of view.

On the other hand, there are two good reasons to place indicators peripherally on a HUD:

1. Peripherally located indicators are less likely to obscure important OTW images (IA-1), which tend to be centrally located (Newman, 1995).

2. There is some evidence that eye motion to periphery of a HUD may discourage attention trapping as indicated in IA-6 (Sanford et al., 1993). This motion can be induced by placing important indicators that are part of a pilot's normal scan out on the periphery of the HUD.

Military standards recommend that airspeed and altitude indicators be separated by at least 10 degrees to give a clear view ahead. However, the standards state that they must remain in the instantaneous field of view and must not be so far apart that cross-check scan time increases (MILSTD, 1996). This generally translates into a separation of about 25 degrees or less. Bank angle, slip/skid, and heading indicators are on the vertical periphery. Only the attitude and attitude-related symbology such as the horizon, pitch ladder, waterline, and CDM are located centrally (MILSTD, 1996). Some civil HUDs locate the heading display centrally, but some experts caution against doing this indiscriminately (Newman, 1995).

Conclusion While the military standard provides a good rule of thumb that has been supported with experience, there is little scientific evidence on the tradeoff between centrality to allow detection of indicator events and the need to keep the OTW view clear.

Even under the assumption that a pilot will learn to regularly scan a key instrument located far from the center, there are arguments against peripheral placement. Peripheral placement of indicators may actually increase the

17

reaction time to centrally-located OTW events that occur while the pilot is scanning the periphery, or may even prevent such events from being noticed. Tradeoffs between indicator size and location complicate the design decision. A large indicator on the periphery, showing a large amount of movement in response to events, may be as visible as a small indicator in the center. Another factor that needs to be taken into account is the possibility that locating an indicator on the periphery reduces the chance of attention trapping.

Centrally locating the attitude indicator is consistent with an argument that the first task of flying is attitude control (which in turn affects speed, heading, and altitude), but no research as specifically tested the need for a dead-center attitude indicator in HUDs. Conceivably, research might show that sufficient attitude awareness and control can be achieved with a non-conformal attitude display (e.g., the "orange peel" as described in Figure 4) presented less than centered (e.g., towards the bottom of the display).

Certification Implications Until more research can be conducted, the military standard of 10-25 degrees of separation for altitude and airspeed is an interim guideline. The attitude indicator may be slightly off-center; provided it is clearly readable when the pilot is fixating on the center of the display.

Future Research This issue is a further elaboration of IA-1 and would be answered by its research. The tradeoff is between interfering with the OTW view and promptly detecting ITD events. In IA-1, the designer may reduce the masking of the OTW view by re-designing the format of the display. In this issue, OTW masking can be reduced to a lesser extent by moving the indicator to the periphery.

Issue **IA-5 Compensation for Lack of Centrality**

Certification Need Determine if adequate compensation is provided for any indication that is too far from the center by creating redundancy in the center (e.g., digital speed, worms).

Importance Low

Findings Commonly HUDs for military and civil application include two centrally located indicators that supplement the airspeed indicator, namely a speed worm and acceleration cue. The acceleration cue combined with a speed worm reduces workload by:

1. Providing lead information for a new airspeed facilitating smoother changes.

2. Representing optimal angle of attack and achievable pitch for current airspeed.

3. Indicating if the aircraft is gaining or losing energy.

4. Providing a control-compatible cue on how to achieve a stabilized airspeed.

18

5. Providing early detection and escape information for windshear (MILSTD, 1996).

These indicators also reduce the importance of the airspeed indicator, making it more reasonable to place it on the periphery. A similar function is performed by the CDM/FPM with respect to vertical speed, which can be inferred from the CDM's relation to the pitch ladder making it less critical to monitor the vertical speed indicator. Flare cues and orange peels (see Figure 4), which are also redundant with other indicators, have also been recommended (Newman, 1995).

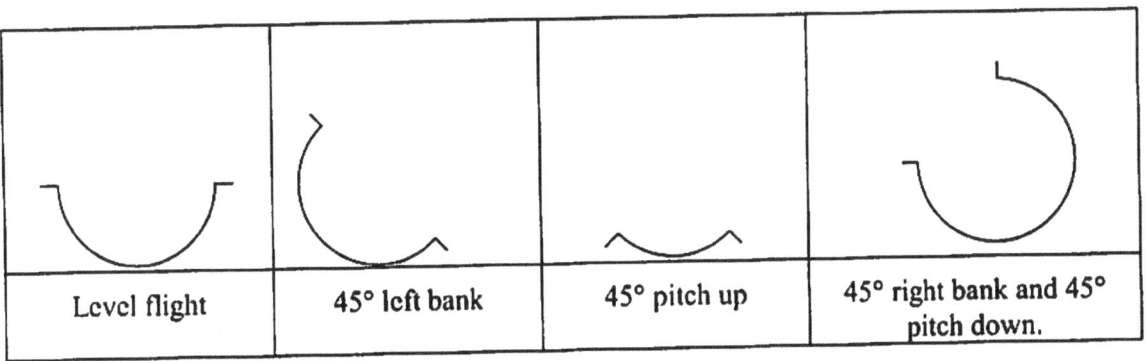

| Level flight | 45° left bank | 45° pitch up | 45° right bank and 45° pitch down. |

Figure 4. A Variation of the Orange Peel.

The completeness of the "peel" indicates pitch, while the orientation of the "handles" indicates bank angle with the gap pointed towards the horizon.

Conclusion The CDM/FPM, speed worm, and acceleration cues are credited with making high-precision manual approaches possible (Kaiser, 1994; Newman, 1995), thus they have earned their place in the middle of the display. But the question for this issue is how does this impact the other indicators? None of these compensatory indicators fully replace the traditional indicators. Speed worms and acceleration cues do not indicate if the airspeed is approaching a performance limit, and are only useful when the pilot has set a specific speed to maintain. The CDM (or vertical component of the FPM) shows flight path angle, confounding vertical speed with air speed.

The traditional indicators thus cannot be eliminated entirely, but these compact compensating indicators suggest that the traditional indicators have diminished importance, which a display may exploit to minimize cluttering effects. For example, can airspeed now be placed further on the periphery or be made smaller? The exact phase of flight may also have an impact. Once stabilized on final approach, a simple digital airspeed indicator may be acceptable when combined with a speed worm, acceleration cue, and some automated approach monitoring and alerting features.

There are other compensations that could be provided in future HUDs. For example, adding a small orange peel to the FPM can make it possible to make the pitch ladder less conspicuous without sacrificing attitude awareness. Unfortunately, there does not appear to be any research providing guidance on how much compensation these indicators provide.

Certification Implications — Until research can determine the compensating effects of these indicators (if any), a conservative approach would be to require that all Basic-T indicators be adequate on their own as to format and location irrespective of the possibility of compensation from other novel indicators.

Future Research — This issue is really an elaboration of IA-4, now with the added element that the information in an indicator may be partially replicated elsewhere on the HUD. It still comes down to determining a satisfactory location for each source of information and it requires research for development.

Issue — **IA-6 Attention Trapping**

Certification Need — Determine the degree the display design sufficiently minimizes attention trapping for the intended tasks.

Importance — Medium

Findings — Among the major benefits of a HUD is that it allows a pilot to read instrumentation while keeping the OTW view in sight and relatively in focus (Weintraub & Ensing, 1992). However, early experiments showed that pilots do not necessarily see the OTW view just because it is in the field of view. Under certain conditions "attention trapping" (or "cognitive capture") can occur in which the perception of OTW events is delayed even though they occur in full view, unobscured by the HUD symbology (Fisher, Haines, & Price, 1980). This appears to be more likely to occur with regard to events that the pilot does not expect, such as a runway incursion while on approach.

The possibility of attention trapping can be mitigated by three strategies:

1. *Eye scanning.* Operational experts argue that training the pilot to scan properly can prevent "tunnel vision" on HUD or part of the HUD: e.g., the FPM and runway symbol (Kaiser, 1994). It appears that eye motion encourages attention shifting between objects including between those OTW and ITD. This could be induced in the HUD's design by spatially separating regularly scanned indicators (Sanford et al., 1993).

2. *Symbology conformity.* There is some reason to believe that conformal symbols tend not to induce attention trapping (Boston & Braun, 1996; McCann and Foyle 1993; McCann, Foyle, & Johnston, 1993; Sanford et al., 1993). In theory, by viewing the symbology in relation to the OTW view, some attention to the OTW view is consistently maintained (Martin-Emerson & Wickens, 1997). However, the capacity of conformity to mitigate attention trapping may not be entirely consistent. May and Wickens (1995) found no difference in the capacity of detecting OTW events between a display with a conformal pitch ladder and heading indicator and a display with a compressed pitch ladder and heading

20

indicator (May and Wickens, 1995). Martin-Emerson and Wickens (1997) likewise found no difference in reaction time to OTW events for their conformal and non-conformal HUDs. However, both of these studies used relatively expected OTW events, which may not be particularly susceptible to the effects of attention capture.

3. *Scene-linked symbology.* Research by NASA suggests that attention capture is primarily due to differential motion between the OTW and ITD elements (McCann and Foyle 1994). Conformity per se will therefore not eliminate attention trapping as a conformal symbol is not necessarily moving with the OTW images (e.g., the pitch ladder frequently appears to move over the ground as the aircraft flies along). These researchers have developed and tested scene-linked symbology (SLS), a type of conformal symbology that moves with the OTW view. ITD objects are painted on the HUD as if they are fixed to the ground, and move past the aircraft as it flies. SLS has been shown to reduce inattention to OTW views when compared to non-conformal symbology (Foyle et al. 1995; McCann and Foyle 1994).

4. *Clutter.* It is reasonably possible that clutter in general may encourage more attention trapping (Boston & Braun, 1996), perhaps by emphasizing the ITD plane at the expense of the deeper OTW view. Martin-Emerson and Wickens (1997) did not observe a significant difference to reaction time to unexpected OTW events between a HUD and an HDD. Their HUD had relatively low clutter while including both conformal and non-conformal elements.

5. *Attention Priorities.* It has been speculated that by reducing the task of landing to a simple but demanding (high gain) tracking task, attention deteriorates for cues other the flight director and FPM. HUD symbology makes it possible to land an aircraft without almost no reference to the OTW scene. As a result, attention on the OTW scene is reduced (Weintraub & Ensing, 1992).

Differential color (McCann & Foyle, 1993) and differential focal lengths (Edgar et al., 1993; Iavecchia, et al,. 1988) for the HUD and OTW have both been proposed as contributing to attention trapping. However, it is possible to get attention trapping effects when controlling for these factors (McCann & Foyle, 1993; McCann & Foyle, 1994).

Conclusion   There is some evidence that conformal symbology reduces attention trapping, but generally the argument is weakly supported by the research. One problem is that much follow-up research has employed relatively expected events, while the research originally detecting attention trapping found it only occurred for unexpected events (Fischer, Haines, and Price, 1980). It may be reasonable that conformal symbology has less of an effect than non-conformal, but it does not eliminate the possibility of attention trapping.

There is a difference between conformal symbology and SLS. If McCann and Foyle (1994) are right and differential motion causes attention trapping, then being conformal alone is not sufficient to prevent attention trapping. Unfortunately, no one has tested SLS against non-SLS conformal symbology. The difference is not merely theoretical. For example, if relative motion causes attention trapping then the attention trapping effects of *non*-conformal symbology can be minimized by placing it where there is little relative motion, namely near the horizon or, for near-ground flight such as landing, up in the sky. However, this would be ineffective if attention trapping is actually avoided by establishing a relation between the OTW and ITD objects through conformal symbology.

Certification Implications   There does not appear to be sufficient consensus how to mitigate attention trapping in order to provide interim guidelines. The weight of the evidence suggests that conformity is desirable, but there is no rule of thumb of how much conformity is necessary. It is important to note that non-conformal symbology (e.g., compressed heading and pitch indicators) have advantages of their own that may outweigh the potential for attention trapping.

At this stage, the best advice is that certifiers should be vigilant for HUDs with high clutter of non-conformal symbology, particularly when presented below the horizon for approaches and landings. Such a HUD may not only be susceptible to attention trapping (owing to large amounts of relative motion, non-conformal symbology, and clutter) but it also is more likely to obscure important OTW objects (see IA-1).

Future Research   What is required is a more definitive study of isolating whether attention trapping is promoted by relative motion or lack of relation between symbology and the OTW view. Once this piece of the puzzle is added, then metric development can proceed. Given that the attention trapping phenomenon is most pronounced for unexpected events, such a metric may be limited to a design evaluation of the HUD symbology or modeling of pilot response rather than a flight test procedure. Flight test pilots, being aware of the procedure, would be difficult to surprise.

The effect of induced eye motion on attention trapping remains an intriguing area of investigation with serious implication on HUD layout.

Issue   **IA-7 HDD Event Perception**

Certification Need   Determine the degree the HUD affects the likelihood of the pilot noticing important events on HDD indications including cautions and warnings.

Importance   High

Findings   The "magnetic" nature of using a HUD has spurred considerable research on the capacity of a HUD to distract the pilot from OTW events (IA-1, IA-6) and even from events within the HUD itself (IA-2). However, it appears no one has studied the possibility that a HUD may inhibit perception of HDD events.

It is known that ITD events are perceived faster with a HUD that with an HDD (Martin-Emerson & Wickens, 1997; Ververs & Wickens, 1998), and this serves as one of the motivations for installing a HUD in the first place. However, it is not known if a pilot is less likely to notice HDD events when using a HUD than when not using a HUD. That is, can a HUD disrupt the normal scan of secondary instruments?

Conclusion Our literature review has not uncovered any publicized incidents of pilots failing to notice HDD events. It is possible that this is not really a problem for HUDs. This has implications for the placement of indicators on the HUD. It may be a reasonable assumption that leaving an indicator on HDD makes it less likely to be noticed than if it is on the HUD, but the degree of this effect needs to be known before engineers consider placing it on the HUD.

Certification Implications At this time, no advice can be given to certifiers.

Future Research Perhaps the first question is to establish the degree this is a problem. A search of the ASRS database for all HUD incidents may be done to determine if this phenomenon exists. Other than this, no other research may be necessary.

If it is a problem, substantial research will be necessary to develop and test a theory for the design characteristics (if any) of the HUD that contribute to the problem. The research for development of metrics for IA-1 and 2 would also bear directly on this issue as the solution may be to move some HDD indicators to the HUD, perhaps using a minimally cluttering format.

Issue IA-8 Cautions and Warnings on HUD

Certification Need Determine that necessary information regarding appropriate warnings and cautions are shown on the HUD so that they are quickly acted upon.

Importance High

Findings As with IA-7, this issue has not been subjected to research. It is recommended, however, that the HUD should generally just repeat master warning/caution annunciation to direct pilot's attention to the HDD (Newman, 1995). FAA flight testing found that a Master Caution annunciation on the HUD was "extremely valuable" in cueing the pilot to check the HDD (Anderson, 1996). It is not known if the HDD master caution annunciator was in plain view on this aircraft when the pilot is using the HUD. Specific messages should be displayed on the HUD only if necessary for safe flight (Newman, 1995).

Conclusion As when using HDD instruments or when flying visually, it seems sufficient for a display to get the pilot's attention and then have the pilot look head down at the appropriate display for more information.

An exception would be warnings on problems that relate directly to aircraft attitude or control where the appropriate display to resolve the problem is the PFD or Basic-T. Assuming the HUD has the appropriate indicators in this

23

case, it should be assumed that the pilot will tend to use the HUD as a PFD, and thus the message should appear on the HUD itself. Windshear, TCAS, and ground proximity are perhaps the best examples of this, and indeed, with a conformal FPM, a HUD may be superior to an HDD PFD for handling these conditions.

Certification Implications Perhaps the same guidelines that apply to HDDs can be generalized to HUDs, namely, that the master warning/caution annunciator must be in detectable view when the pilot is looking at the HUD. This annunciator may be either HDD (e.g., on the glareshield) or in the HUD to satisfy this guideline. Given that most HDD master warning/caution annunciators are presumably designed to be easily noticed when the pilot is looking OTW in VMC flight, it is likely the HDD annunciator will already be sufficient on most aircraft.

However, certifiers should verify that the annunciator is easy to perceive during actual use of the HUD and that the HUD hardware, such as the combiner frame, does not interfere with the view of the annunciator. A HUD repeater annunciator, which replicates the PFD or master warnings and cautions on the HUD, may not be required, but it is generally desirable as it assures quick detection while adding little clutter (given that it is rarely on and is removable by such means as pilot acknowledgement).

As for specific messages, a reasonable approach is that any message that appears on the HDD PFD should also appear on the HUD. Also, any message that can be effectively resolved through the use of the indicators on the HUD should also be on the HUD.

Future Research It may be a good idea to test if an HDD master is equally noticeable in VMC when not using a HUD as when using a HUD for certain tasks. This would test if HUDs tend to especially focus attention away from the HDD. The question of whether the master warning/caution annunciation belongs in a particular HUD design can be covered under the research on the allocation of indicators between the HUD and HDD (IA-7).

Other than that, it may be reasonable to assume that noticing cautions and warnings is not a problem, and this issue can be closed without any further research.

Issue **TD-1** Attribute Guidelines

Certification Need Determine compliance of the uses of symbology attributes (such as brightness, ghosting, flashing, positioning, boxes, underlining, "---," "XXX") with their preferred use.

Importance High

Findings Coding can be done using color, size, shade or brightness, weight or boldness, frequency (dashed, dotted, and ghosted symbols), symbology shape (e.g., font, pointer appearance), overlaid shapes (underline, overscoring, boxing, circling, X-ing, strikethrough), adjacent symbols (e.g., asterisks, arrows, icons), motion

24

(flashing, shifting/alternating, throbbing, inverting, looming), and position.

Based on a cursory review of HDDs, the following dimensions have relatively consistent coding across air transports PFDs. These would constitute the dimensions available for coding for a HUD:

1. Armed vs. engaged settings, as in autoflight modes. Color and position coded on the PFD, with typically engaged modes over armed. Color varies by aircraft.

2. Performance limits (e.g., pitch, speed). Color, shape, and/or frequency coded on PFD. The use of red and stripes (e.g., "barber poles") seem to be most common.

3. Out-of-range ("pegged") values. Position coded, often displayed at extreme of an indicator scale.

4. Not applicable or no data (e.g., autoflight mode). Shape coded, e.g., dashes.

5. Warning vs. caution vs. advisory. Color coded and position coded, with the top and red for warning, and yellow or amber for caution.

6. Horizontal vs. vertical (as on the PFD). Position coded, horizontal and speed on the left, and vertical on the right.

7. Mode capture. Typically coded with adjacent symbols or overlaid shapes.

Some recommend that removal of the indicator symbology is sufficient to indicate a fault in the indicator (Newman, 1995). However, removal of symbology was associated with significantly slower reactions to failures than overlaying X's on the indicator (Liggett & Hartsock, 1993). This lead to the USAF standard to overlay a box and X on a failed indicator. After pilot acknowledgement, the faulty indicator is then removed (MILSTD 1996). Some civil HUDs overlay a boxed alphanumeric annunciator on the indicator (Flight Dynamics, 1999). The performance difference, if any, between this convention and the military standard is unknown.

The military standard and other HUDs use both frequency ("ghosting") and position to indicate out-of-range parameter values. The horizon and the FPM are ghosted if their positions go out of the HUD's field of view, with the position indicating the direction towards these indicators in a manner consistent with that used for HDDs (Flight Dynamics, 1999; MILSTD, 1999). An out of range commanded airspeed and altitude is shown above the airspeed and altitude indicators, respectively (Flight Dynamics, 1999; MILSTD 1996), a convention also seen on some HDDs.

The military standard marks speed limits with adjacent symbols (letters) rather than a frequency-oriented method used in HDDs and some other HUDs (Flight Dynamics, 1999; MILSTD 1996; Newman, 1995).

The position coding of horizontal and vertical information is generally upheld in HUDs (Flight Dynamics, 1999; MILSTD 1996; Newman, 1995).

Motion such as flashing is very effective at drawing the pilot's attention, but tends to be distracting and makes the symbology or message difficult to read. It is recommended that flashing only be used as a general attention-getter and that it not have any other dimension coded with it (e.g., warning vs. caution or indicator failure) (Newman, 1995; Society of Automotive Engineers, 2000).

Color is a favorite code for HDD instruments (e.g., PFDs and NDs), although beyond cautions vs. warnings and sky vs. ground, there are sharp differences in how color is used. Color is not available on current HUDs and, although some high end HUDs may soon have color, one can expect monochrome HUDs to be in service for some time to come. The apparent color on a HUD is also affected by colors of the OTW view in the background, making color an unreliable coding method for HUDs.

While a clear distinction can be made with electronic HDDs between shade (e.g., gray versus black lettering) and weight (e.g., normal vs. bold lettering), the two may be more easily confused on a HUD.

Differential boldness or brightness has been suggested as a means to distinguish essential and nonessential symbology in order to reduce the effects of clutter (Ververs and Wickens, 1998). This would remove this coding method from the list of alternatives. See IA-1 and IA-2.

Conclusion   X's or other overlays are the preferred to removal or ghosting an indicator to show an indicator failure. Assuming the pilot can remove the overlay and indicator, this is probably worth the clutter temporarily added by the overlay.

Ghosting is becoming a de facto convention for representing an out-of-range indicator, and it appears to be performing well in that capacity.

The best use of flashing probably is purely to capture the attention of the pilot.

The use of alphanumeric symbols rather than some other symbology (e.g., stripes) to represent limits is suspect owing to the occasionally ambiguous meaning the letters may have (e.g., "M" may mean either "Maximum" or "Minimum"). However, research is needed to investigate this suspicion.

In general, there is a lack of broad criteria to evaluate an arbitrary coding scheme for cautions, warnings, and performance limits.

Certification   Ghosting, flashing, and removal of symbology are not recommended to
Implications   indicate a failed indicator. Overlaying with X's is known to work well. Other methods may work equally well. Flashing may be used as an attention getter as long as it does not persist for more than a few seconds.

While there are some *de facto* HUD conventions and some HDD conventions that can and have been extended to HUDs, no guidance can be provided for handling HUDs that deviate from these conventions if there are good reasons

26

(e.g., less clutter). There is no research showing the magnitude of the effects of such deviations on pilot performance.

Future Research HUDs are capable of matching the conventions for HDDs for all coding methods except color. Research should focus on developing a means to evaluate a monochrome coding conventions for those dimensions that depend on color on HDDs. Chief among these is the color-coding for cautions and warnings, which may be extended to the coding of performance limits. This is probably the most important and consistently used coding on HDD instruments. This represents a fairly modest research effort.

Automation modes also frequently use color, but not nearly so consistently, and position alone may be adequate coding.

Issue **TD-2** Sky-Ground Discrimination

Certification Need Determine adequacy that HUD distinguishes sky from ground in order to recognize unusual attitudes.

Importance Medium High

Findings While traditional HDD attitude indicators use relatively large areas of color and shade to distinguish sky from ground, HUDs are hampered in this by a lack or color and a need to minimize clutter (Weintraub & Ensing, 1992). The sky and ground can be symbolically distinguished through differences in the appearance of the positive and negative bars on the pitch ladder. Pitch bars can differ in size, gap size, weight, color (when it becomes available), use of tapering, use of articulation, use of dashing, tick mark position, or any combination of the these (Dudfield et al., 1995; Newman, 1995; Previc, 1989).

For performance purposes, tapering or articulated pitch bars may go either on the top or bottom, as long as some sort of pitch ladder vertical asymmetry is employed (Weinstein et al., 1994). However, pilots prefer articulated rungs on the bottom rather than on top (Weinstein, et al., 1993), and this has become a standard for the USAF (MILSTD, 1996).

The MIL-STD 1787B standard symbology was found to be as good as a standby HDD for UA recovery (Weinstein, et al.1994). Specifically, pilots using the military standard recognized and responded to a UA within 1.5 seconds (Society of Automotive Engineers, 2000). This symbology uses four differences in positive and negative pitch bars to distinguish sky from ground: solid vs. dashed lines, articulation vs. straight bars, inside rung tips vs. outside, and single-sided labeling, which when combined with horizon pointing ticks can serve as a cue (MILSTD, 1996).

Caution should be employed if articulated pitch ladder rungs are used. When combined with an uncaged pitch reference (e.g., the FPM), pilots make more errors in initiating a recovery from unusual attitudes. This is probably due to false roll axis cues produced by the articulated rungs. (Weinstein et al., 1993; Newman, 1995).

27

Color can be used to indicate negative vs. positive pitch ladder. In laboratory tests, traditional blue/brown coding works best, but in real world these may be hard to see against the natural OTW blue and brown backgrounds (Dudfield et al., 1995; Newman, 1995).

Zenith and nadir symbols provide additional sky-ground discrimination (MILSTD, 1996, Newman, 1995). However, these will rarely cue transport pilots because of the HUD's relatively limited field of view. Transports are very unlikely to assume an attitude that would bring these symbols into sight even in the most severe upset. Thus, while useful, zenith and nadir symbols cannot be relied on alone.

There are additional means of providing pitch information in a more compact and holistic way than a pitch ladder. These include *le boule*, the orange peel (see Figure 4, Page 19), grapefruit (a big orange peel), and the theta ball (Newman, 1995; Previc, 1989, Ercoline & Cohen, personal communication).

Conclusion   The pitch ladder has the fundamental problem that pilot must distinguish sky and ground by picking off fine attributes of symbology that are likely to be moving. It is very similar to the problem of trying to read the numbers from a moving tape indicator. As a result, the military's experience suggests that several differences in the positive and negative pitch ladder rungs are necessary for a HUD to match a HDD for sky-ground recognition.

Alternative means of providing pitch information, such as the orange peel, do not have the problems of pitch ladders. However, unlike the pitch ladder, they have the disadvantage of being non-conformal even at normal attitudes, and this has advantages (see IA-1 and IA-6).

Certification Implications Based on the research to date, the following guideline is recommended.

HUD pitch symbology should be displayed such that the following are true:

1. Sky and ground are clearly differentiable under all conditions including those involving rapid changes in pitch or roll. This can be accomplish through either of the following:

    1.1. The negative and positive pitch ladder rungs are differentiated on multiple dimensions. The negative sign for the negative pitch labels does not qualify as a difference.

    1.2. The HUD provides a clear, graphic indication of the general direction and extremity of the pitch that is readable during upsets, unusual attitudes, and all rapid maneuvers (e.g., an orange peel).

2. Articulated ladder rungs should only be used with a caged FPM or CDM.

3. Clearly differentiable nadir and zenith symbols should be used.

In order to minimize clutter, the HUD may be programmed to automatically alter the pitch indicator to comply with this guideline when the aircraft enters an unusual attitude.

Ultimately, actual pilot performance should be used to evaluate the effectiveness of sky-ground discrimination. Latency of control input and percent of correct initial control inputs can be used as metrics of display performance. See TD-5.

Future Research Currently, researchers are comparing alternative pitch indicators for effectiveness in maintaining flight path and recovering from unusual attitudes (Cohen & Ercoline, personal communication).

The interim guideline of simply recommending "multiple" differences between positive and negative pitch bars is rather crude and fails to take into account that some differences are more compelling than others. Research is needed to arrive at a more precise measure. Since a metric only has to predict the discrimination of sky from ground, there is currently sufficient knowledge to develop a metric for this.

While a metric for design evaluation may be helpful for designers, for certifiers flight testing in this case provides a more direct indication of the effectiveness of the symbology. Using methodology similar to that used by Cohen and Ercoline (see TD-5), testers can determine if the HUD allows detection of, and effective recovery from, usual attitudes.

Issue **TD-3 Instrument Format**

Certification Need Determine appropriateness and adequacy of instrument format (tape, pointer, drum, counter) implementation where any important losses associated with the format are sufficiently compensated by some means.

29

Importance High

Findings For altitude and airspeed, three formats have made their way onto HUDs: fixed pointer linear tapes, round-dial pointers combined with digital counters ("counter-pointer"), and digital counters. In most studies, counter-pointers performed as good or better than tapes. Counter-pointers were associated with better speed and altitude maintenance and higher ratings by pilots than tapes or purely digital indicators (Ercoline & Gillingham, 1990; Weinstein et al. 1993; Weinstein et al. 1994). While pilot-evaluators gave acceptable ratings to counter-pointers for both airspeed and altitude, they gave lower ratings for altitude tapes, apparently due to difficulty in detecting slow deviations from a target altitude. Speed tapes were rated equal to or above speed counter-pointer (Anderson, French, Newman, & Phillips, 1995)

In principle, the tape altitude and airspeed indicator has the following advantages over the counter-pointer:

1. The absolute difference between current values and reference values are easier to see, owing to the labeling of the tick marks.

2. A finer division of values and greater display gain is possible within the same display area for a given range of values

3. Position of current value relative to reference values is unambiguous.

The last point pertains to the fact that for counter pointers, when the reference value is near the opposite side of the dial, it may be more difficult to determine if the current value is above or below the reference value. It is not known if there have been any actual incidents of confusion of this sort. Current HUD designs only show the reference value when it is less than a semicircle away from the current value (i.e., 40 knots or less for airspeed and 400 ft or less for altitude). Thus, pilots can use the rule that the reference value is always "the short way around" from the current value (MILSTD, 1996). The alleged effect could also be mitigated by a means of drawing a connection between the current value and the proper direction towards the reference value (clockwise or counterclockwise), although at the cost of more clutter.

The counter-pointer, meanwhile, has the following general advantages over tape (Kantowitz & Sorkin, 1983; Newman, 1995; MILSTD 1996; Weintraub & Ensing, 1992):

1. Easier to read at a glance because the numbers are not slewing and the needle orientation provides an approximation of the current value

2. Provides unambiguous trend information that is analogous to ordinary HDD round dials (e.g., with a tape altimeter, downward motion on the indicator means the aircraft is ascending).

3. Easier to distinguish rate and direction of trend during extremely rapid changes.

30

The counter-pointer also have the following advantages when specifically used on a HUD:

4. Less clutter and space on the display, reducing the chance of obscuring the OTW view.

5. Does not give misleading attitude cues (i.e., the preponderance of vertical and horizontal lines in tapes can act as pseudo-pitch ladder rungs or horizons; opposite motion of the tapes can generate the impression of a roll occurring).

6. Motion of the indicator is not counteracted by the apparent motion of terrain.

This last advantage may have been responsible for the superior altitude maintenance observed with counter-pointers. The apparent ground motion from changes in pitch associated with altitude changes can become synchronized with the slewing of the altitude tape, masking the tape's motion. This is probably a real effect whose consequences have been observed in flight tests of actual aircraft (Anderson, et al., 1995). However, it should be pointed out that the experiments of Ercoline & Gillingham, (1990) Weinstein et al. (1993), and Weinstein et al. (1994) may have unrealistically exaggerated this effect due to the particular terrain texturing they used in their simulators (Ercoline, personal communication).

The effects of tapes providing misleading attitude cues is most critical during unusual attitudes. This effect can therefore be mitigated by an automatic decluttering mechanism (Newman, 1995) that replaces the tapes with simple counters during unusual attitudes. A similar decluttered mode can be made available to pilots for VMC when an unobscured outside scan is most needed (Flight Dynamics, 1999).

The rate information provided by an analogue display such as a pointer or tape is important to pilots. Pure counter displays may be used in certain decluttered modes such as for VFR flight, but are not recommended for standard use (Newman, 1995). This is also true for vertical speed indicators. Compared to a counter display, vertical speed tracking is superior with an analogue vertical speed indicator, especially if it is in close proximity to altimeter (e.g., as found with MILSTD vertical velocity arc). Pilots prefer that a counter still be displayed combined with the analog indicator (Weinstein et al., 1993; Weinstein, et al., 1994).

Conclusion It is apparent that counter-pointers are as good or better than tapes, although it appears possible to make a tape that out-performs the counter-pointer for certain tasks (e.g., speed maintenance). In general, analog indicators have important performance advantages over simple counters although counters alone may be appropriate for situations when the absolute minimal clutter is necessary.

Some of the advantages of counter-pointer over tapes apply as much to HDDs as HUDs. Other advantages peculiar to HUDs may be mitigated or exaggerated. To the degree that tapes have become acceptable for HDDs, one may regard them as adequate for HUDs even though counter-pointers may represent a better overall engineering compromise.

Certification Implications
To the degree that tapes are considered to be adequate for certification, research indicates that counter-pointers should also be regarded as acceptable, and this issue may be considered closed with the conclusion that either counter pointer or tapes are acceptable if properly implemented.

Proper implementation implies the same guidelines that apply to any important indicator (e.g., that values are clearly readable, that the scale be linear, that order and motion are compatible with pilot expectations). Displays of any format should have evenly spaced tick marks, although they can be very small, being just detectable.

When evaluating tape airspeed and altitude indicators, certifiers should specifically check for the following:

1. Carefully flight check the capacity of the pilot to maintain an altitude in VMC conditions.

2. Check for misleading attitude cues when the aircraft is in unusual attitudes. Recommend automatic removal of these cues from the tapes when entering unusual attitudes if such cues are problematic.

3. Evaluate for tendency to obscure important OTW objects when in VMC. Recommend a decluttered (counter only) VMC mode be made available to the pilot, if clutter is a problem.

When evaluating a counter-pointer airspeed and altitude indicators, certifiers should specifically check for the following:

1. Tick marks are at round values in intuitive or expected units so that labeling is not necessary. Recommend sparse labeling if units are nonintuitive for some pilots.

2. The relative positions of the current values to commanded and reference values are always unambiguous.

A digital-only format for Basic-T indicators and vertical speed may be allowed for a decluttered mode, but the pilot should always have the means to quickly bring up analogue indicators when needed (e.g., using a switch on the control column).

Future Research
No further research is necessary to determine if tapes or counter-pointers are adequate for use on a HUD. No metric is necessary. Another question concerns the mixing of formats between the HUD and the HDD. This question is addressed by DD-4.

Issue	**TD-4** Limits and Target Values
Certification Need	Determine if the display adequately indicates and distinguishes commanded values and limits in altitude and speed displays.
Importance	High
Findings	The military standard uses unlabeled carets for commanded values on both the airspeed and altitude indicators. Reference values are shown with the same caret combined with a single letter label (e.g., G for gear retract speed) (MILSTD, 1996). HUDs using fixed-pointer tape indicators show limits with striped bands in a manner analogous to that seen on electronic HDD PFDs (Flight Dynamics, 1999).
Conclusion	There does not appear to be any research on HUDs regarding symbology that would best distinguish target values and limits. There is also apparently no research on the actual symbology of reference speed markers. Most HUDs show a reference speed as a symmetrical symbol, similar to the mechanical bugs on non-electronic instruments. For certain indicator formats (e.g., the military-style counter pointer), it may be ambiguous from a momentary glance whether the aircraft is converging on or diverging from the reference value. For certain reference speeds, such as stall speed, the "right" side of the reference value is not necessarily clear.
	It would seem reasonable that the same guidelines that have been applied to electro-mechanical and electronic HDDs be also applied to HUDs, with the absence of color being the only real difference. For HDD indicators, the right and wrong sides are indicated by coding a range of values with color or pattern. A similar thing could be done with HUDs or, in order to minimize clutter, simple symbol asymmetry could be employed to the same effect. The value of these remains untested for the present. See TD-1.
Certification Implications	Certifiers may apply the same guidelines for HDDs to HUDs when evaluating the HUD. If a limit or value must be displayed on the PFD HDD, then the same should be displayed on the HUD in a manner analogous to that used successfully for HDDs (excepting for the use of color). The HUD representation may be more compact than the original HDD version in the interest of minimizing clutter (see IA-1). In general, commanded values and out-of-limit ranges of values for an indicator must be readably identifiable and distinguishable.
	See also TD-3 for recommendations regarding the display of reference values on counter- pointers.
Future Research	See TD-1
Issue	**TD-5** Unusual Attitude Recovery

33

Certification Need	Determine if the HUD clearly and directly represents extreme attitudes (possibly through decluttering mechanisms).
Importance	Medium
Findings	Military experience has found that improperly designed HUDs appear to be associated with disorientation during extreme attitudes that can hamper recovery to a normal attitude (Chandra & Weintraub, 1993; Taylor, 1990). Among the reasons given for HUDs contributing to spatial disorientation are the following (Iavecchia, et al., 1988; Newman, 1995; Taylor, 1990):

1. The use of compensatory rather than pursuit displays.

2. Confusion over fly-to versus fly-from formats.

3. Failure to use frequency separated displays (rather than inside-out or outside-in).

4. Indicator format, with some blaming the use of round-pointer dials (Taylor, 1990) and others blaming the use of tapes (Newman, 1995).

5. Incompatibility with the HDD (e.g., between track-up HSI and heading-up HUD).

6. The use of air mass rather than inertial FPMs when on approach (Taylor, 1990). On the other hand, an air mass FPM provides more aerodynamic information than an inertial FPM, which is very useful in unusual attitudes (Newman, 1995).

7. Attention trapping.

8. Simulation of an electro-mechanical attitude indicator's precession at zenith and nadir.

9. Pilots treating the FPM as a pitch marker rather than a performance indicator.

10. Differences in accommodation between the HUD and the OTW view.

11. Clutter and the excessive concentration of information.

Perhaps the biggest factor that prevents a HUD from performing as well as a traditional HDD attitude indicator in recovery from unusual attitudes is the relatively truncated pitch scale it displays. While a HDD "eight ball" attitude indicator displays at least 40 degrees of pitch scale, the limited field of view of a HUD restricts a conformal pitch ladder to only 30 degrees or less. Thus, only a small part of the scale is visible at once, and it may slew by too quickly for the pilot to recognize the direction of pitch (Newman, 1995; Weintraub & Ensing, 1992).

Whatever way the HUD contributes to a failure to recover from unusual attitudes (UA), the most direct method to mitigate the effects is to simply train pilots to use HDD indicators in the event that they ever encounter a UA

(Lyddane, personal communication). The HUD, in that case, only needs to adequately alert the pilot of a UA (see TD-2).

There are advantages to using the HUD for UA recovery however. Going head down requires that the pilot re-accommodate and re-orient to the HDD indicators, delaying recovery action. In a military aircraft, the pilot may have to call up the HDD attitude on a multifunction display with a stick or yoke switch, further delaying recovery and introducing the possibility of a switching error.

Efforts to make a HUD adequate for UA recovery have focused on enhancing or augmenting the attitude information the HUD provides. Slight pitch scale compression (1.5:1 to 2:1) improves tracking performance and UA recovery, but landing, takeoff, and terrain avoidance are better with conformal scale (Haworth & Newman, 1993). Thus, some HUDs are designed with variable pitch compression with conformal pitch ladder rungs near the horizon (for normal flight) and compressed rungs at extreme pitches (Flight Dynamics, 1999; MILSTD, 1996; Newman, 1995).

Other efforts have focused on indicating the direction of pitch motion relative to the horizon. Frequently, the tips of the pitch ladder rungs are turned to point to the horizon (Flight Dynamics, 1999; MILSTD, 1996; Newman, 1995), and this has proven to be very effective for most situations (Chandra & Weintraub, 1993). When in extreme negative pitch, transport pilots can recover quickly by rolling until the tips point up (relative to the pilot's head) and then pulling up. For extreme positive pitch, the transport pilot pitches down in the direction of the tips and then rolls level to complete the recovery (*Aero*, 1998).

Anything on the ladder rungs, however, may be too difficult to use for certain dynamics such as spins (Chandra & Weintraub, 1993). Thus, other UA recovery cues have been proposed which can be automatically displayed when the aircraft enters a UA. Among these are (Chandra & Weintraub, 1993; Newman, 1995; Weinstein et al., 1993; Weinstein, et al,. 1994):

1. Horizon or zenith pointing devices on the CDM/FPM, such as ghost horizons (see TD-1) and Augie Arrow (see Figure 5).

2. Compact, holistic attitude indicators, such as the orange peel (see Figure 4, Page 19).

Along with presenting UA recovery cues, the HUD can also automatically declutter the display, addressing another potential factor in the inhibition of effective UA recovery (Newman, 1995; Society of Automotive Engineers, 2000). Ratings by pilot-evaluators suggest that this is helpful (Anderson et al., 1995; Anderson, 1996). When a UA is encountered, one transport HUD replaces the ordinary conformal pitch ladder with a large "theta ball," i.e., a wireframe version of the traditional HDD attitude indicator (Proctor, 1999).

Properly implemented, a pilot can perform UA recoveries equally well with a HUD as with a standby head-down attitude indicator (Fullmer, personal communication; Weinstein, 1994). Specifically, pilots using the military standard HUD recognized and responded to an UA within 1.5 seconds and their initial inputs were correct over 90% of the time (Society of Automotive Engineers, 2000). The military standard achieves this through the use of pitch ladder compression, horizon-pointing tips on the rungs, articulated rungs (for negative pitch only) and a ghost horizon (MILSTD, 1996).

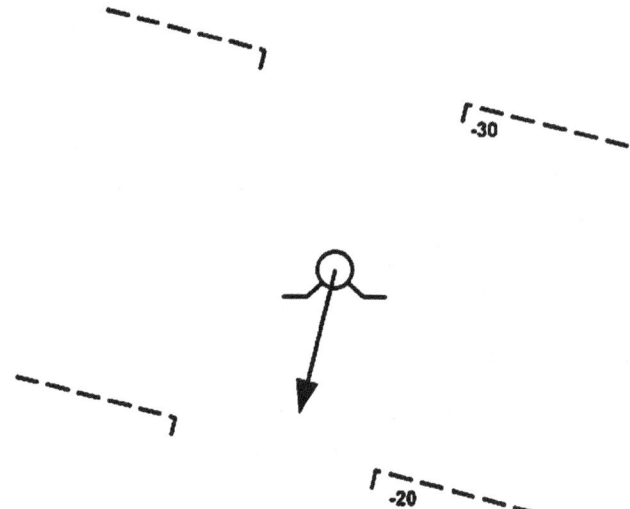

Figure 5. Hypothetical Application of an Augie Arrow to a Civil-Styled FPM.

The arrow points towards either the horizon or zenith depending on the design. The symbology indicates that this aircraft is inverted.

Conclusion   With a HUD providing adequate orientation cues and decluttering, a pilot can use a HUD to effectively recover from a UA. Other factors that have been suggested to contribute to disorientation when using a HUD while in UA have not been addressed by research.

Certification   If a HUD is intended or expected to be used to recover from UA, then research
Implications   suggests that the HUD should have the following:

1. Symbology that provides clear and obvious cues to general orientation in all possible attitudes and upsets at all times. Horizon-pointing tips on the pitch ladder alone are not sufficient. However, more than one form of symbology may be employed to satisfy this guideline. For example, horizon-pointing tips on the pitch ladder rungs may be presented at all times while an Augie Arrow or a ghost horizon may be presented during a UA when the pitch ladder may not be sufficiently readable.

2. The form of this symbology must be compatible with the UA recovery response expected of the pilot for all possible UA's.

3. If a pitch ladder is the primary source of pitch value to the pilot, then the pitch ladder should have compression at extreme attitudes of a least 1.5:1 for large (about 20 degree vertical or more) field-of-view (FOV) HUDs.

36

Greater compression is needed for smaller HUD FOVs.

4. The display should automatically declutter in the event of a UA. No more than the Basic-T and symbology necessary to effect UA recovery should be displayed. It is acceptable that the HUD software also automatically remove or simplify elements of the Basic T other than altitude (e.g., heading).

5. There should be no simulation of the precession at zenith and nadir that is necessary on electro-mechanical attitude displays.

It is assumed that pilots will receive training for using the HUD for UA recovery.

While the above guidelines may be useful for designers to develop a HUD that allows effective UA recovery, for certification purposes flight testing in a simulator provides a more direct evaluation. Following a procedure from military experiments (Ercoline, personal communication) and experience (Fullmer, personal communication; Society of Automotive Engineers, 2000), a test pilot is exposed to various unusual attitudes. Latency and correctness of response is measured. Latency of initial control input should be 1.5 seconds or less and the input should be correct at least 90% of the time (Society of Automotive Engineers, 2000).

See TD-3 for more on decluttering in the event of a UA for HUDs that use tape indicators.

See TD-2 for additional certification implications that apply to both HUDs that are and are not used for UA recovery.

Future Research The advent of such devices as Augie Arrow may have effectively solved this problem for UA and no further research is necessary. If one wanted a metric to *compare* different designs, one could try using the display gain of the pitch and roll indicator for orientation towards horizon or sky. This metric could be validated in an experiment measuring reaction time and error rate (or number of control reversals) for the initial control column input in response to an unusual attitude. However, rather than deriving a metric from design characteristics, it may prove to be more reliable to simply use flight tests to compare competing designs.

It may still be worth investigating the suggested factors 1 through 11 on Page 34 to see if they can also contribute to disorientation, perhaps in non-UA conditions. For both design and training purposes, it may also be of interest to determine under what sorts of displays or conditions pilots can more effectively recovery from UA by switching to HDDs.

Issue **DD-1 Internal Consistency**

Certification Need Determine consistency in the use of coding (shape, size, position) and attributes to provide information separation, discrimination, and categorization.

Importance High

Findings   While the importance of consistency is known (e.g., Society of Automotive Engineers, 2000), there does not appear to be any research on consistency in HUD codings, nor is there apparently research on formal methods to determine inconsistency or the amount of inconsistency humans can tolerate.

Conclusion   Conventional wisdom is that any inconsistency is undesirable and unnecessary and should thus be eliminated. This, however, does not address situations when inconsistency may be necessary. There may even be human factors reasons for an inconsistency, where in making a HUD indicator consistent with closely related control, it becomes inconsistent with other HUD indicators. It would seem reasonable that under certain situations a pilot can tolerate such an inconsistency within a HUD if the inconsistency is between two very separate functions. The literature, however, does not provide guidance on how to make this judgment.

Certification Implications   Given the lack of research on consistency of codings in HUDs, the following are recommendations concerning the general subjective evaluation of internal consistency:

1. The evaluation for internal consistency begins with a review of the manufacturer's stated coding scheme. Any of the following within the coding scheme are causes for concern and candidates for redesign.

    1.1. The same meaning with two different codes on two different indicators. This is the less serious form of inconsistency. The seriousness increases with (a) an increasing relatedness or similarity of the two indicators, and (b) a decreasing similarity in the two codes.

    1.2. The same code having two different meanings on two different indicators. This is the more serious form of inconsistency. The seriousness increases with (a) an increasing relatedness or similarity of the two indicators, and (b) a decreasing similarity in the two meanings.

2. After evaluating the coding scheme, the actual display implementation is evaluated for compliance with the manufacturer's stated coding scheme. Any deviations from the coding scheme are candidates for redesign.

3. Finally, the rationale and compensation for each inconsistency are evaluated. An inconsistency may be necessary or even desirable for various reasons (e.g., in order to maintain external consistency with another closely related display or control). The benefits of having the inconsistency must be weighed against the seriousness of the inconsistency. An inconsistency can be compensated by such means as using labeling and redundant coding.

It is assumed that the pilot will be educated on the coding scheme used by the HUD.

Future Research   There is a basic lack of research in human factors on how to measure inconsistency and how much inconsistency humans can tolerate before performance deteriorates. Answering this question requires formal definition, theory building, and metric development regarding inconsistency. This can be somewhat simplified by limiting the study to design variations present on contemporary HUDs.

Once one has a validated measure of inconsistency, one can conduct experiments on the performance impact of various levels of inconsistency in order to determine the level of inconsistency that is associated with an operationally significant decrement in performance. The entire program is likely to require long-term in-depth research.

Issue **DD-2** Basic T

Certification Need Determine significance and acceptability of certain deviations from the Basic-T layout, allowing for certain deviations if offset by certain gains.

Importance High

Findings Apparently, no one has conducted experiments to evaluate the actual impact of moving the heading indicator to the top of the HUD, although it is fairly common practice going back to some of the earliest HUDs (MILSTD, 1996; Newman, 1995).

The primary rationale behind relocating the heading indicator to the top is that it leaves the lower portion of the display relatively unobscured, providing a clear view of the ground where hazards or targets (e.g., terrain, runways, incursions) are more likely. There is also reason to believe that attention trapping is more likely if the HUD displays the heading indicator overlaying the ground as Basic T would require (Sanford, et al., 1993; Foyle et al., 1995).

When the heading indicator is placed above the artificial horizon, the bank indicator tends to be placed below, where its behavior is more compatible (e.g., a bank to the right corresponds to the pointer moving to the right). The bank indicator is frequently a simpler and less cluttering indicator than the heading indicator, making the former an obvious choice for this space on the HUD.

Extensive military experience using a number of different HUDs plus flight testing of civil HUDs suggests that having the heading on top presents no consistency problems (Anderson et al., 1995, 1996; MILSTD, 1996; Newman, 1995).

There is some evidence that rotorwing craft would benefit from swapping the positions of speed and altitude in an effort to seek better control display compatibility (Newman, personal communication). But so far no civil HUDs have been designed in this manner.

Conclusion In limiting the issue to just the vertical position of the heading indicator, the key research question is to determine the performance cost of a pilot re-acquiring the heading information when switching to HDD. Although there is no research on this, it would seem unlikely that a pilot would confuse the attitude indicator for a heading indicator given that they appear so different. Therefore, the most likely performance cost would be a delay on the order of a fraction of a second in acquiring the heading information. This does not sound like an excessive cost given the advantages of a top-placed heading indicator on the HUD. Flight experience implies that this indicator placement is not a problem, and perhaps on this basis alone, this issue may be closed.

The same cannot be said for any other deviations in the Basic T (e.g., swapping airspeed and altitude, where the potential for confusing one indicator for the other is greater). Certainly, if a rotorcraft HUD or helmet-mounted display were to show altitude on the left and airspeed on the right, then a similar arrangement for the HDD would seem to be necessary. However, it is unlikely that any manufacturer would propose such a deviation for a fixed-wing transport, and this question is perhaps beyond the scope of this project.

Certification Implications As an interim guideline, positioning the heading indicator over the attitude indicator is acceptable on a HUD. Any other deviation from the HDD arrangement of the Basic-T is not acceptable.

Future Research It would be a fairly straightforward test to determine the effects of transitioning between alternative heading indicator positions. This will not produce a metric per se, but it will provide a simple yes-no answer whether locating the heading indicator above the attitude display has any operational significance. Given that extensive flight experience suggests that it does not, one may chose to forego even this modest study. See also DD-4.

Issue **DD-3** Caution-Warning Discrimination

Certification Need Determine if cautions displayed in the HUD are distinguishable from warnings.

Importance Medium Low

Findings While flight testing suggests there are advantages to repeating the master caution/warning display on the HUD (Anderson, 1996; Newman, 1995), apparently many HUD installations do not provide such annunciations, limiting warning messages to just those specific to the HUD itself (Flight Dynamics, 1999; MILSTD, 1996; see IA-8). For HUDs with caution/warning annunciator repeater, no research has been conducted on the importance or means of distinguishing cautions from warnings.

Conclusion Research is lacking in this area. With regard to the HUD master caution/warning repeater, it would seem reasonable that the word "CAUTION" and "WARNING" are themselves sufficient to distinguish cautions from warnings and that no additional coding is necessary. However:

1. The HDD master annunciator uses color coding, evidently with important attention-drawing effect, and thus an analogous non-verbal technique is called for in the HUD.

2. A coding scheme is still necessary for messages that do not contain the

words "CAUTION" and "WARNING" (e.g., "WINDSHEAR"), and internal consistency requires that such a scheme be applied to the master repeater too.

One approach is to catalogue the techniques that have been shown to result in identification reaction times as fast as can be achieved with color. However, this would not allow evaluation of techniques that have not been invented yet. As with TD-1 (see Page 24) there is a need to develop criteria or guidelines for evaluating a convention that distinguishes cautions from warnings in a monochrome display. This issue would thus be subsumed under TD-1 as any criteria developed shall be tested for discrimination.

Certification Implications   If a HUD displays cautions and warnings, then some means should be employed to help the pilot clearly and immediately distinguish among warnings, cautions, and advisories. The codings should be readily distinguishable when viewed in isolation and should indicate increasing seriousness from advisory through caution to warning. This could be done through increasing the number, size, or weight of a feature of the annunciator.

Finally, the code for warning and caution and the position of the annunciator must be such that the pilot perceives it immediately. However, the use of flashing should be avoided to distinguish warnings from cautions for this annunciator unless other means are not effective in drawing the pilot's immediate attention (See TD-1, Page 24).

Future Research   See TD-1

Issue   **DD-4 External Consistency with PFD**

Certification Need   Determine adequacy of consistency between formats of HUD and PFD for flight indications and for rapid adjustment by the pilot when transitioning between the two under a worse case scenario.

Importance   High

Findings   As a general human factors principle, it is desirable to seek stimulus-stimulus compatibility among related displays (Kantowitz & Sorkin, 1983; Woodson, 1992). This does not mean that two displays must necessarily be identical, but only that their behavior must not contradict each other. For example, if round dial pointer displays are used for altitude on both the HUD and the HDD, then, if one shows increasing altitude in a clockwise direction, the other must as well. Unfortunately, beyond this general principle, there does not appear to be any systematic research on mixed format types.

It has been recommended that both HUD and HDD display essentially the same information, but it is deemed acceptable, when there is adequate justification and subsequent pilot evaluation, for the form of the information to be different (Society of Automotive Engineers, 2000). The HDD may differ from the HUD in compression, format, and display modes. Many successful implementations have mixed round dial with tapes between the HUD and the HDD. Flight tests indicate that pilots do not have a problem switching from the FPM/CDM referenced HUD to a pitch-marker/attitude referenced HDD. Use of the FPM on the HUD should not lead to problems if the pilot mistakenly uses the same techniques for flying by reference to the pitch marker on the HDD. It is not necessary for HDD and HUD indicator formats to match (Newman, 1995).

Conclusion The conventional wisdom that the displays can be different as long as they do not contradict is hard to refute but somewhat difficult to interpret in practice. Based on flight experience, it would seem acceptable to mix a fixed-pointer tape indicator with a round-dial moving pointer indicator for the same parameter. There may even be advantages to mixing the two formats in the same cockpit as each may be more suitable for certain tasks or pilots, and supplying both simultaneously gives the pilot some degree of choice.

However, there are other combinations of formats that could be interpreted as violations of the stimulus-stimulus compatibility principle. An example is combining an HDD fixed pointer moving tape indicator with a HUD moving pointer fixed scale indicator. As the parameter value increases, the pilot is confronted with downward motion in the HDD and an upward motion in the HUD. It is not known how pilots will react to this.

Certification Implications Based on experience with prior HUDs, it is not required that the HUD and HDD match on indicator formation. It is acceptable to combine a round-dial with a tape. However, certain combinations which may present contradictory behavior should be carefully flight tested. This includes combining of fixed pointer tapes with moving pointer linear scales, and combining moving card round dial with moving pointer round dial.

Future Research Research should focus on determining the difficulties a pilot can experience when transitioning between the basic indicator formats. It is entirely possible that there are no serious problems when making such transitions. A relatively modest study could determine this and perhaps obviate the need to develop a metric.

Issue **DD-5 External Consistency with Cautions and Warnings**

Certification Need Determine sufficiency of similarity between HDD cautions and warnings and those on the HUD.

Importance High

Findings There has apparently been no research specifically studying consistency between the display of alerts such as cautions and warnings on HUDs and on HDDs.

In a brief review of cockpit caution and warning annunciators, cautions and warnings are distinguished primarily by color, which most HUDs are not capable of producing and would not be adequate in any case because the

42

underlying OTW view can change the apparent color of a HUD symbol (Society of Automotive Engineers, 2000). The only other coding that is occasionally used is by position with warnings shown above cautions.

See DD-3 for other relevant general findings regarding alerts on HUDs.

Conclusion Like DD-4, general human factors guidance suggests that the design goal is that the HDD alert attributes must not contradict the HUD alert attributes. For example, if underlining is used for cautions while bold is used for warnings on the HDD, then the HUD must not use the opposite. This leaves open the possibility of the HUD using an entirely different coding scheme (as may be necessary given that HUDs are generally monochromatic). This is an inconsistency of sorts although it is generally considered minor, one that may lead to an additional training burden but usually not operational confusion (see DD-1).

The analysis of TD-1 proposes that criteria be developed to evaluate monochromatic conventions be developed for warnings and cautions. If this is done, then the import of DD-5 is that the proposed criteria must consider potential contradictions the coding scheme used for HDDs. Given that the only common non-color HDD code is relative position, this should be easy to accomplish.

Certification Implications While it is desirable for both HDD and HUD alerts to use the same coding scheme, general human factors practice suggests that it is acceptable for HUD alerts to use a different coding scheme than HDD alerts as long as they do not contradict each other. If HUD alerts are coded using the same dimensions as the HDD alerts (e.g., both code by relative position), then the HUD must use the same coding scheme (e.g., if the HDD displays warnings above cautions, then the HUD must also).

Future Research See TD-1

Issue **PS-1** Effects of Strain on Performance

Certification Need Evaluate characteristics of the HUD to determine if the physiological strain of using a HUD disrupts performance for the intended use.

Importance Medium

Findings The potential exists for HUDs to cause more physiological strain than comparable HDDs, where such strain may be manifest by general fatigue, eye fatigue (eyestrain), difficulty focusing, or skeletal-muscular tension. Conceivably, these symptoms may result from the usual or unnatural optical qualities associated with collimation and superimposition of images.

There has apparently not been any systematic research on the effects of strain from using a HUD although there are anecdotes of pilots experiencing eyestrain from extended HUD sessions in the simulator. There is some evidence that the

43

shift of attention from the HUD to the OTW view requires a change of focus despite the use of collimated displays (Edgar et al., 1993), which could contribute to strain. However, one would not expect it to be any greater than that experienced by a pilot who is shifting attention between an HDD and the OTW view in an non-HUD-equipped aircraft.

In practice, pilots voluntarily use HUDs in VMC conditions when it is not necessary for visibility purposes (Kaiser 1994). This would not occur if physiological strain were pronounced. However, continued HUD use during long-range operations has not been investigated.

Conclusion The strain effects of HUDs remain a possibility, although currently they are unsubstantiated.

Certification Implications The strain effects of HUDs are unknown. In test flights, evaluators should use HUDs for the expected duration of use in order to evaluate any strain effects.

Future Research To start with, one should first survey pilots on their subjective strain. If more strain is reported for using the HUD than the HDD, then further research is needed to determine the source of strain (e.g., optical distortions, focusing difficulties, eye box restrictions). This could ultimately result in a complex long-term study.

Issue **PS-2** Minimal Optical Quality

Certification Need Determine adequacy of optical quality in order to prevent excessive fatigue and eyestrain.

Importance Medium

Findings There are apparently no published papers on HUD optical quality and eye fatigue or strain. As stated with PS-1, no strain or fatigue effects associated with using HUDs have been documented so far. This, however, does not mean that a manufacturer seeking to produce a low-end HUD cannot make one whose optical quality has strain or fatigue effects. It is hypothesized that collimation imperfections could lead to errors in distance estimates to OTW targets (Weintraub & Ensing, 1992).

Conclusion Published sources do not provide any guidance on the optical quality necessary to prevent strain and fatigue, or even what physical dimensions or characteristics of HUD optics are related to strain or fatigue. This issue is closely related to PS-1 and could be treated jointly with it.

Certification Implications See PS-1.

Future Research It is necessary to interview HUD optical engineers to see how they addressed this issue. Such engineers, along with vision experts, would provide the background necessary to know what HUD physical characteristics might induce fatigue or strain. These physical characteristics could then be manipulated experimentally to determine the levels that produce unacceptable fatigue or strain. This would become part of the research program used to address PS-1.

Issue **PS-3** Cockpit Head Motion Volume (CHMV)

Certification Need Determine adequacy of size of cockpit head motion volume in order to prevent flight indications on the periphery from going out of view with normal head movement.

Importance High

Findings Based on experience developing HUDs for the military, Newman (1995) recommends a 4x4x2 inch (LxWxH) rectangular volume for transports to allow for reasonable head motion. Given that a warplane's canopy frequently restricts head motion substantially, it is possible that a larger space is needed for transports to accommodate normal head motion. The Society of Automotive Engineers recommends a slightly smaller 4x3x2 inch volume based on operational air transport experience (Society of Automotive Engineers, 2000). On the other hand, for the primary tasks that HUDs support in air transports, namely approach, landing, and takeoff, natural head motion may be very low. The actual amount of head motion to expect for various tasks is unknown.

Conclusion While clearly the larger the better, making a large CHMV is technically difficult for HUD manufacturers, making this a contentious issue. But despite the attention applied to this issue, there is remarkably little hard data on relevant pilot behavior.

Flight experience suggests that the CHMV in current HUDs is sufficient for the brief periods of approach, landing, and takeoff. However, HUDs may be increasingly used for long periods while en route. For this application, if the HUD is to be the sole primary flight reference, then the CHMV may have to be considerably larger. It may even be discovered that HUDs cannot be currently built to have an acceptably large CHMV in order to serve as the sole PFR for cruise, and thus an HDD PFD must be provided with the HUD.

Certification Implications While guidelines such as Newman's exist for manufacturers, these are not based on rigorous scientific study. Thus, HUD evaluators must rely on flight testing to determine if the CHMV seems sufficient. Evaluators should not have to excessively restrict head motion in order to see all key indicators simultaneously while performing the tasks the HUD was designed to support. Evaluators should not experience unacceptable muscle fatigue, cramping, or other physical effects from attempting to hold the head excessively still.

Future Research There are several questions that are relevant to this issue:

1. What is the natural amount of head motion a pilot exhibits during the tasks a HUD may be used for?

2. What is the normal amount of deviation from the cockpit design eye point

45

exhibited by a diverse population of pilots with a wide range of physical dimensions?

3. It may be acceptable that certain less important indicators (e.g., DME) can be positioned such that they occasionally require head motion even when the pilot's eyes are in the CHMV. What can be defined as the "key indicators" that must be in continuous view for the entire CHMV?

4. Is it sufficient for a key indicator to be visible with only one eye?

The logical starting point is to tackle the first question above and measure the amount of normal head movement associated with the tasks a HUD is used for. This alone may be sufficient to provide a guideline for CHMV.

Issue **PS-4** Accommodation

Certification Need Determine if the design of the HUD will cause excessive adverse vision effects (fatigue/workload or delays) in adjusting to new focal lengths and brightness when switching to HDD indications for the intended uses of the HUD.

Importance Medium

Findings While collimation theoretically places the HUD image at optical infinity, laboratory studies indicate that people may actually be focusing at much less than infinity when using a HUD (Edgar et al., 1993; Iavecchia, et al. 1988). The near-focusing on the HUD may account for some cases of misjudgments of OTW sizes and distances when using a HUD, as incorrect focus is associated with errors in size estimations (Iavecchia, et al. 1988). However, when a person looking through a HUD shifts attention from the HUD symbology to the OTW scene, focus increases to about infinity, suggesting that OTW objects are in focus when a pilot attends to them (Edgar et al., 1993). Furthermore, a collimated HUD tends to draw focus further out than a comparable HDD, requiring less accommodation when shifting gaze to the OTW scene (Weintraub & Ensing, 1992).

There is some evidence that people focus farthest from infinity when the HUD is viewed against a featureless background. This would imply that pilots experience accommodation shifts as they fly into or out of clouds. Some speculate that these shifts in focus could account for reports of disorientation when flying through clouds owing to changes in retinal image size (Iavecchia, et al., 1988). However, the effect of focusing on retinal image size is controversial and may even be in the opposite direction hypothesized by Iavecchia (Weintraub & Ensing, 1992).

The shifts in focus experienced between the HUD and the OTW may occur only when the HUD uses non-conformal symbology. This was indicated by irregular decreases in lateral flight path deviations when pilots flew an ILS approach into and out of IMC while using a non-conformal HUD. Pilots using a conformal

46

HUD exhibited uniform decreases in deviations as they entered and exited IMC conditions while closing on the localizer (Martin-Emerson & Wickens, 1997).

Conclusion In the case that pilots do not appear to be focusing at infinity when using the HUD, they will generally not be required to make major focal accommodations when transitioning to the HDD. The effects of adjusting to differential brightness have apparently not been investigated, but it would seem reasonable that the adjustment is no greater than for a pilot transitioning between the OTW view and the HDD during VMC in a non-HUD aircraft.

Research, however, suggests that pilots probably do shift focus (and attention) when transitioning between the HUD and the OTW view. This may be true for non-conformal symbology only, although this has not been demonstrated yet. The existence of this shift of focus has not been fully established due to methodological limitations of the existing research. For example, Iavecchia, et al., (1988) used a backlit linen sheet one meter away from subjects to simulate IMC. The possibility exists that the close range of the sheet led to the subjects focusing closer.

Even less established are the consequences of such a shift in focus. No link has been made, for example, between these shifts in focus and eye fatigue. It has not been established that changes in focus are the cause of spatial disorientation or errors in distance estimations, or that these problems are more pronounced when using a HUD-equipped aircraft than a non-HUD-equipped aircraft (where clearly a shift in focus is necessary between the HDD and OTW). Disorientation associated with flying through clouds is a poorly understood phenomenon but it is known to occur with non-HUD aircraft as well. Given that focus shifts together with attention when the pilot looks OTW, focus-induced distance errors should be unlikely when using a HUD in actual operations. Differences in focal distance may contribute, among other factors, to attention trapping (see IA-6), but this has yet to be demonstrated in the laboratory.

Certification Implications At this time, the existing research is too preliminary to provide certification guidance. While it is reasonable to assume that pilots generally do not necessarily focus at optical infinity when using the HUD, the implications of this statement on performance have not been established, and the means to ameliorate it are still speculative.

Future Research A research-for-development effort can be justified in this area, first focusing on replicating the results under conditions closer to actual flight and establishing the performance deficits (if any) that are due to the focusing effects. Possible negative effects include:

- Fatigue

- Disorientation

- Increased workload

- Errors in distance estimation

- Increased reaction time for traffic detection

These initial studies could be followed by research into the means to counteract these effects, starting with measuring focusing distances when using a conformal HUD where the symbology is used in conjunction with the OTW view (e.g., when lining up the FPM on the runway threshold in VMC). Studies into improving the optics may also be in order (see PS-2).

5. PROPOSED RESEARCH PROGRAMS

In reviewing the Future Research sections for the issues in Part 4 of this document, it may be noted that many issues require research for metric development. Resolving most of the remaining issues can be accomplished through relatively simple studies, but these studies tend not to provide quantitative metrics. For these issues, no quantitative metric is necessary in order to provide useful certification guidance.

One research program frequently can resolve more than one issue. For example, many of the IA issues can be resolved by developing a means of evaluating the effectiveness of the display of information on the HUD.

Table 2 below identifies how the research for each issue can be consolidated into eight main programs. Each program is described in the final sections of this document. In the table, an entry of "*none*" for the Program column indicates that no additional research is required to resolve the issue. Other issues that may require no additional research are IA-7, IA-8, DD-2. However, useful information for these issues may be derived from programs required to resolve other issues. These programs are given in parenthesis.

Table 2. Research Programs for the Design Issues.

Issue		Program
IA-1	Clutter Effects on the OTW View	Visual Scanning
IA-2	Clutter Effects On HUD Use	Visual Scanning
IA-3	Minimal Information Display	Visual Scanning
IA-4	Centrality of Indicators	Visual Scanning
IA-5	Compensation for Lack of Centrality	Visual Scanning
IA-6	Attention Trapping	Conformity vs. SLS
IA-7	HDD Event Perception	(Visual Scanning)
IA-8	Cautions and Warnings on HUD	(Visual Scanning)
TD-1	Attribute Guidelines	Alert Coding
TD-2	Sky-Ground Discrimination	*none*
TD-3	Instrument Format	*none*
TD-4	Limits and Target Values	Alert Coding
TD-5	Unusual Attitude Recovery	*none*
DD-1	Internal Consistency	Internal Consistency
DD-2	Basic T	(HDD-HUD Consistency)
DD-3	Caution-Warning Discrimination	Alert Coding

Issue		Program
DD-4	External Consistency with PFD	HDD-HUD Consistency
DD-5	External Consistency with Cautions and Warnings	Alert Coding
PS-1	Strain Effects on Performance	HUD Strain
PS-2	Minimal Optical Quality	HUD Strain
PS-3	Cockpit Head Motion Volume	Head Motion
PS-4	Accommodation	HUD Strain

The following sections of this document describe each research program. For each program, the following is given:

- **Issues Addressed.** The issues the program seeks to resolve. This is the same information as in the Table 2 re-organized by program.

- **Resources.** Indicates resources necessary for the research. "Simple" indicates that relatively modest resources are necessary usually implying that a single study is called for. "Long-term" indicates that more extensive resources are necessary, usually implying that literature searching, theory building, and multiple studies are required.

- **Metric.** Indicates whether the research is expected to yield a validated quantitative metric of the HUD design that may be used by certifiers in their evaluations. A "No" indicates that the program will yield a general qualitative conclusion (e.g., on the acceptability of a particular design).

5.1 Visual Scanning

Issues addressed: **IA-1 through IA-5, IA-7, IA-8.**

Resources: Long-term

Metric: Yes

The purpose of this research program is to develop a metric to determine if a HUD adequately balances minimizing clutter against providing sufficient and easily accessible information to the pilot. The metric is expected to represent the total "cost" in time and visual effort for the pilot to acquire all necessary information from the HUD and the OTW scene (Carbonell, 1966). The cost of acquiring a particular type of information, for example, the current altitude, is a function of the following:

- The ease with which the pilot can shift his or her eyes to the information source. This may be proportional to how far the source is from the center of the pilot's field of view (e.g., the distance from the center of the HUD to the altimeter).

- The interference caused by other information sources. This "clutter factor" is expected to be related to the amount and form of other nearby sources (e.g., interference between the altimeter and other indicators and important areas of the OTW scene).

- The frequency the pilot must acquire the information to maintain safe and proper operation. This is proportional to the probability that the information source displays something that the pilot must respond to (e.g., an altitude deviation).

The data for the last item can be gathered for a given task by surveying pilots, subject matter experts, or the existing literature manual control literature (e.g., Clement, Jex, and Graham, 1968).

We can validate the metric by measuring, in a simulator. flight control precision and pilot reaction time to events that occur both OTW and ITD. For example, for IA-1, pilots fly various different HUD layouts in a simulator and the reaction time to respond to traffic conflicts is measured. As the combined cost of using all the information sources increases (as indicated by the metric), the reaction times should also increase. Measuring the excessive dwell time or insufficient sampling in pilots' scan patterns can also be used for validation. HUDs with either too much or too little information may result in inadequate cockpit scan patterns, increasing the likelihood of missing significant events. Scan patterns can be measured in a simulator with an eye tracker device. Possibly, the scan pattern may become more disordered as elements of a display become difficult to detect or read. There are several methods available for deriving a score for orderliness of scan patterns from these data (Hacisalihzade et al., 1992; Stephens, 1981).

5.2   Conformity vs. SLS

Issues addressed: **IA-6**

Resources: Long-term

Metric: Yes

The ultimate aim of this research program is to create a metric for a HUD symbology's propensity to promote attention trapping. To do this, experiments must be run to determine if non-conformal symbology or relative motion cause attention trapping, as current research is not conclusive on this. The experiment compares reaction time to unexpected events for HUD using Foyle and McCann's (1995) scene-linked and non-scene-linked conforming symbology. Such a study must include both expected and unexpected events and control for clutter.

The results of the experiment can indicate the appropriate metric for measuring a HUD's propensity to induce attention trapping. If attention trapping is caused by relative motion, then the metric is the amount of relative motion between HUD and OTW for a particular task. This can be directly measured knowing the dimensions and placement of the symbology and the probable attitude and above ground altitude of the aircraft.

If attention trapping is caused by non-conformal symbology, then the metric is the amount of non-conformal symbology. This can be measured a number of ways, but as a simple first approximation, absolute angular area covered by non-conformal symbology could be used. Some

51

allowance may be made for non-conformal symbology that is compressed rather than completely unrelated to the OTW view.

For either alternative metric, relative motion or non-conformity, the relevant symbology should probably be weighted by frequency of use by the pilot, the latter determined empirically or by task analysis.

To provide validation, the metric is correlated with reaction time to unexpected OTW events such as the appearance of traffic or obstacles. Another possibility is to measure flight path deviation cued by the OTW scene while the pilot performs a HUD-related task.

5.3 Alert Coding

Issues addressed: **TD-1 TD-4, DD-3, DD-5**

Resources: Simple

Metric: Yes

The purpose of this study is to develop guidelines for effective non-color coding conventions for cautions and warnings. The guidelines would be developed to help those who must evaluate how HUD designs identify and distinguish caution and warning indications (TD-1 and DD-3) and for operationally significant regions on indicators (TD-1 and TD-4). The development of these criteria and guidelines will consider how non-color coding methods are currently used on HDDs (DD-5). Non-color methods include:

- Weight, e.g., caution is twice as heavy as normal and warning is thrice as heavy.

- Frequency, e.g., "…" is caution and "///" is warning.

- Adjacent Symbols, e.g., "!" for caution and "!!" for warning; perhaps "◎" for limits.

A workshop of aviation experts is convened which surveys existing avionics to identify and assess the effectiveness of candidate conventions for non-color coding of cautions and warnings. Both good and poor conventions are identified. From these are derived more general guidelines for potentially effective designs.

To provide validation, an experiment compares subjects' reaction times for correct identification of warnings, cautions, and normal conditions, testing exemplar conventions that follow the guidelines and exemplars that do not. Adequate performance for an exemplar convention would be that equal to or better than a color convention control condition. The guidelines are considered validated if they discriminate successfully the exemplar conventions with adequate performance from those without.

5.4 Internal Consistency

Issues addressed: **DD-1**

Resources: Long-term

Metric: Yes

The purpose of this research program is to develop a metric for internal consistency of the codings and conventions of a set of indicators in a display. As a first approximation, it is hypothesized that the potential for confusion between two different codings on two different indicators varies with the following:

1. Confusion increases with the relatedness between the indicators.

2. Confusion increases with the discrepancy between the similarity of codings and the similarity of the meanings of the codings.

For example, a hypothetical HUD may use bold print to mean an *engaged* autopilot mode. A major inconsistency would be to use bold print for *armed* autothrottles because:

1. Autopilot and autothrottle are closely related.

2. While the coding (bold print) is the same (high similarity), the code meanings are dissimilar. Thus the difference between the coding similarity and the meaning similarity is high.

Similarly, for autothrottles to use normal print for *engaged* would also represent an inconsistency for the coding of *engaged*:

1. Autopilot and autothrottle are closely related.

2. The coding (bold vs. normal) is very dissimilar (low similarity), while the code meanings are the same (high similarity). So again the absolute difference between the coding similarity and the meaning similarity is high.

In conjunction with the autopilot example, a less serious inconsistency would be to use bright print to mean *standby* radio frequencies. Here:

1. Autopilot mode and radio tuning are relatively unrelated.

2. The meaning of *engaged* and *standby* while dissimilar, are not as dissimilar as *engaged* and *armed* (although the higher similarity between *engaged* and *in use* would suggest that they should be coded similarly). The codes of boldness and brightness, while similar, are not identical. Thus the difference between the coding similarity and the meaning similarity is moderate.

The total amount of internal inconsistency for an indicator on a display can be found by comparing all of its codes and meanings to the codes and meanings of all other indicators on the display. To do this, similarity scores are needed for each code pair and meaning pair, and a relatedness value is needed for each indicator pair. This can be empirically derived by surveying pilots.

The metric is validated in an experiment measuring reaction time and error rate in identifying the meaning of codes on various indicators.

5.5 HDD-HUD Consistency

Issues addressed: **DD-2, DD-4**

Resources: Simple

Metric: No

This study investigates the pilot performance cost associated with making the transition between a HUD and HDD when each use different formats or locations of indicators. This is done using a desktop part task simulator with the computer screen divided into two displays with the subject pilot performing a tracking task using the indicators. At random intervals, one display is turned off and the other is turned on, forcing the subject pilot to make the transition between the two. Disruptions in flight path are recorded. Eye motion is also recorded throughout the experimental trial to provide clues to the cognitive nature of any disruptions observed.

To address DD-2, a 2x2 experiment independently varies scale geometry (round or linear) and pointer motion (fixed or moving). To address DD-4, a 2x2 experiment varies the location of the heading indicator (either above or below the attitude indicator) in both displays. The outcome of the experiment can provide immediately usable qualitative results, perhaps indicating to certifiers and HUD designers what combinations of formats do not work well together. Recommendations of acceptable combinations of formats would become a design guideline that can be expected to cover nearly all cases for some time.

However, while the above experiment would cover round dial, tapes, thermometer, and other indicator formats, it would not provide guidance for any truly novel indicator that are as yet unimagined. To cover such cases, a more abstract, possibly quantitative, metric must be developed as a follow up to the above experiment. It is challenging to develop a quantitative metric for the contradiction between two different indicator formats. However, if a quantitative metric is desirable, then the above experiment is the first step in metric development. For example, it is entirely possible that transitioning between a fixed and a moving pointer is only problematic if both indicators have the same scale geometry. This would set certain constraints on what qualifies as a "contradiction."

5.6 HUD Strain

Issues addressed: **PS-1, PS-2, PS-4**

Resources: Long-term

Metric: Yes

The first study in this program determines if HUD usage is associated with any more strain than HDD usage. This can be determined by surveying pilots on subjective strain as they complete simulator training and/or on-the-line use of the HUD. These results are compared to matched sample of pilots who use HDD for matched tasks. If no significantly different strain is revealed, then no further research is necessary for this program.

If the survey indicates that HUDs are associated with more strain than HDDs, then more studies are needed to evaluate the relation of eyestrain to actual flight performance. For example, flight path deviation or reaction time to ITD events can be checked. The reasoning is that if the HUD use does indeed fatigue the eyes, then pilots may begin to avoid using the HUD, and the result would be deviation from the flight path in manual flight, or delays in detecting deviations from commanded flight.

If a thorough check of pilot performance fails to show any impact of HUD-induced strain, then the research program ends. On the other hand, if the links between HUD strain and performance are established, then further research attempts to determine the HUD design features that promote or reduce strain. Among these is the need for focal accommodation, although accommodation may have other adverse effects as well.

5.7 Head Motion

Issues addressed: **PS-3**

Resources: Simple

Metric: Yes

Under the best of conditions, the HUD CHMV should be large enough to accommodate normal pilot head motion associated with the task the HUD is used for. Thus, the primary research goal for this program is to determine the range of normal head motion exhibited by pilots in non-HUD equipped aircraft. This would serve as the ideal CHMV for HUD-equipped aircraft. Compact instrumentation makes it possible to measure head motion in a simulator or a actual aircraft in flight. It would also be informative to measure the head motion when a HUD is used to see if pilots are reducing their normal head motion in order to use today's HUDs. All measurements should be done under various environmental conditions, especially turbulence, and perhaps considering a range of cockpit layouts.

The observed 95% head motion volume (as a first approximation) may itself become a guideline for the recommended CHMV. However, it is possible that a smaller volume can be tolerated. Pilots may need to keep their head more still in a HUD-equipped aircraft, but this may not have any adverse impact. Thus, after determining the normal amount of head motion, a follow-up study determines the effects on performance of attempting to restrict this motion for various periods of times. In the extreme case, the pilot is unable to maintain the head in the restricted volume, resulting in indicators dropping from view, and, subsequently, flight path deviation or delays in recognizing ITD events. However, even mild restriction may result in discomfort and fatigue that may affect performance in other ways.

6. SUMMARY

This document provides a literature review of design issues encountered by the FAA during the certification of HUDs for use in air transports. This review extracts certification advice from the literature and identifies research necessary to provide more complete certification guidelines for HUDs. There are four categories of design issues: information accessibility (clutter), task-display compatibility, display consistency, and physiological effects.

There is substantial research on clutter-related issues related, especially with regard to interference with the OTW view. However, while qualitative certification advice can be drawn from these studies, there is a need for a more systematic means to determine an acceptable tradeoff between accessible flight information and clutter. There is also substantial knowledge on the task-display compatibility issues, especially concerning unusual attitude recovery. However, important benefits would be realized from the development guidelines for monochrome coding conventions for information such as alert levels. Research is needed on display consistency, especially regarding the effects of differences between the HDD and HUD layouts and formats. Likewise, the effects of HUD hardware design on pilot physiological stress and performance require study. For example, the amount of head motion a HUD must allow for is not empirically known.

REFERENCES

Anderson, M. W. (1996). Flight test certification of multipurpose head-up display for general aviation aircraft. *Journal of Aircraft* 33(3): 532-538.

Anderson, M. W., Acree, J. N., and Newman, R. L. (1995). *Civil certification of head-up displays*. Los Angeles, CA, Society of Automotive Engineers, 952037.

Anderson, M. W., French, D. D., et al. (1995). Flight testing a general aviation head-up display. *Journal of Aircraft* 33(1): 235-238.

Boston, B. N. and Braun, C. C. (1996). Clutter and Display Conformality: Changes in Cognitive Capture. *Proc. of the Human Factors and Ergonomics Society 40th Annual Meeting*, Philadelphia, PA.

Bradley, P. (1996). Dials versus tapes. *Business and Commercial Aviation*: 70-74.

Carbonell, J. (1966). A queueing model of many-instrument visual sampling. *IEEE Transactions on Human Factors in Electronics*, HFE-7(4).

Chandra, D. and Weintraub, D. J. (1993). Design of head-up display symbology for recovery from unusual attitudes. *Proc. of the Seventh International Symposium on Aviation Psychology*.

Clement, W. F., Jex, H. R., and Graham, D. (1968). A manual control-display theory applied to instrument landings of a jet transport. *IEEE Transactions on Man-machine Systems*, MMS-9(4).

Dudfield, H. J., Davy, E., et al. (1995). The effectiveness of coding collimated displays: An experimental evaluation of performance benefit. *Proc. of the Eighth International Symposium on Aviation Psychology*.

Edgar, G. K., Pope, J. C. D., et al. (1993). Visual accommodation problems with head-up and helmet-mounted displays. *Display Systems*, Munich, FRG, SPIE--The International Society for Optical Engineering.

Ercoline, W. R. and Gillingham, K. K. (1990). Effects of variations in head-up display airspeed and altitude representations on basic flight performance. *Human Factors Society 34th Annual Meeting*, Orlando, FL, Human Factors Society.

Federal Aviation Administration (1987). *Transport Category Airplane Electronic Display Systems* (FAA Advisory Circular 25-11). Washington, DC: Federal Aviation Administration.

Fisher, E., Haines, R. F., and Price, T. A., (1980). *Cognitive Issues In Head-Up Displays* (NASA Technical Paper 1711). Moffett Field, CA: NASA Ames Research Center.

Foyle, D. C., McCann, R. S., et al. (1995). Attentional issues with superimposed symbology: Formats for scene-linked displays. *Proc. of the Eighth International Symposium on Aviation Psychology*.

REFERENCES (cont.)

Hacisalihzade, S. S., Stark, L. W., and Allen, J. S. (1992). Visual perception and sequences of eye movement fixations: A stochastic modeling approach. *IEEE Transactions on Systems, Man, and Cybernetics*, 22(3), 474-481.

Haworth, L. A. and Newman, R. L. (1993). *Test Techniques for Evaluating Flight Displays.* Ames Research Center: 1-15.

Huntoon, R. B., Rand, T. W., and Lapis, M. B. (1995). Outside scene obscuration by a millimeter-wave radar image on a HUD. *Proceedings of SPIE -The International Society for Optical Engineering 2463* 173-182.

Iavecchia, J. H., Iavecchia, H. P., et al. (1988). Eye accommodation to head-up virtual images. *Human Factors* 30(6): 689-702.

Johnson, W. W. and Kaiser, M. K. (1995). Perspective imagery in synthetic scenes used to control and guide aircraft during landing and taxi: Some issues and concerns. *Proceedings of SPIE -The International Society for Optical Engineering 2463* 194-204.

Kaiser, K. J. (1994). *Improved operational reliability and safety with HUD -The Alaska Airlines experience.* Los Angeles, CA, Society of Automotive Engineers.

Kantowitz, B. H. and Sorkin, R. D. (1983). *Human Factors: Understanding People-System Relationships.* New York: John Wiley & Sons.

Leger, A., Fleury, L., and Aymeric, B. (1996). Some human factors issues in enhanced vision systems: An experimental approach through stimulation techniques. *Proceedings of SPIE -The International Society for Optical Engineering 2736* 183-193.

Liggett, K. K., Reising, J. M. et al. (1993). *Failure Indications on a Head-Up Display.* Seventh International Symposium on Aviation Psychology.

Martin-Emerson, R. and Wickens, C. D. (1997). Superimposition, symbology, visual attention, and the head-up display. *Human Factors* 39(4): 581-601.

May, P. A. and Wickens, C. D. (1995). The role of visual attention in head-up displays: Design implications for varying symbology intensity. *Proc. of the Human Factors and Ergonomics Society 39th Annual Meeting*, San Diego, California.

McCann, R. S., Foyle, D. C. et al. (1993). Attentional limitations with head-up displays. *Proc. of the Seventh International Symposium on Aviation Psychology*, Comumbus, Ohio.

McCann, R. S. and Foyle, D. C., et al. (1998). *An Evaluation of the Taxiway Navigation and Situation Awareness (T-NASA) System in High-Fidelity Simulation..* Society of Automotive Engineers, 985541.

McCann, R. S., Andre, A. D. et al. (1997). Enhancing taxi performance under low visibility: Are moving maps enough? *Proc. of the Human Factors and Ergonomics Society 41st Annual Meeting*, Albuquerque, NM.

REFERENCES (cont.)

McCann, R. S., Foyle, D. C. (1994). *Superimposed Symbology: Attentional Problems and Design Solutions*. Los Angeles, CA, Society of Automotive Engineers 942111.

MILSTD (1996). MIL-STD 1787B Aircraft Military Symbology, United States Air Force.

Newman, R. L. (1995). *Head-Up Displays: Designing the Way Ahead*, Hants, England: Ashgate Publishing,.

Previc, F. H. (1988). Towards a physiologically based HUD symbology. Brooks Air Force Base, TX, USAF SAM.

Proctor, P. (1997). Economic, safety gains ignite HUD sales. *Aviation Week and Space Technology*: 54-57.

Proctor, P. (1999). Enhanced head-up symbology builds situation awareness. *Aviation Week and Space Technology*.

Sanford, B. D., Foyle, D. C., et al. (1993). *Head-Up Displays: Effect of Information Location on the Processing of Superimposed Symbology*. Seventh International Symposium on Aviation Psychology.

Society of Automotive Engineers (2000). *Transport Category Airplane Head-up Display (HUD) Systems*. (ARP5288) Warrendale, PA: Society of Automotive Engineers.

Stephens, A. T. (1981). Instrument scan, performance, and mental workload in aircraft pilots. In *Department of Aeronautics and Astronautics*, Cambridge, MA: Massachusetts Institute of Technology.

Taylor, C. N. (1990). *The HUD as a primary flight instrument*. Long Beach, CA, Society of Automotive Engineers, 901833.

Tole, J. R., Stephens, A. T., et al. (1983). Visual Scanning Behavior and Pilot Workload. Hampton VA, NASA Langley Rearch Center.

Ververs, P. M. and Wickens, C. D. (1996). The effect of clutter and lowlighting symbology on pilot performance with head-up displays. *Proc. of the Human Factors and Ergonomics Society 40th Annual Meeting*, Philadelphia, Pennsylvania.

Ververs, P. M. and Wickens, C. D. (1998). Head-up displays: Effects of clutter, display intensity, and display location on pilot performance. *The International Journal of Aviation Psychology* 8(4): 377-403.

Weinstein, L. F. and Ercoline, W. R. (1993). Standardization of Aircraft Control and Performance Symbology on the USAF Head-Up Display. Brooks Air Force Base, TX, United States Air Force.

Weinstein, L. F., Gillingham, K. K., et al. (1994). United states air force head-up display control and performance symbology evaluations. *Aviation, Space, and Environmental Medicine*. 65: A20-A30.

REFERENCES (cont.)

Weinstein, L. F., Ercoline, W. R., et al. (1992). Head-up display standardization and the utility of analog vertical velocity information during instrument flight. *International Journal of Aviation Psychology* 2(4): 245-260.

Weintraub, D. J. and Ensing, M. (1992). *Human Factors Issues in Head-up Display Design: The book of HUD.* CSERIAC State-of-the-art report SOAR 92-2.

Will, B. (1998). HUDs get ahead. *Flight Deck International '98*: 18-21.

Woodson, W. E., Tillman, B., and Tillman, P. (1992). *Human Factors Design Handbook* (2nd ed.). New York: McGraw-Hill.